Praise for *Autism on a Shoestring Budget*

Autism on a Shoestring Budget is an extremely practical guide to help one understand the challenges a parent of a child with autism often deals with. This book contains a treasure trove of examples, from social stories and visual supports to guidelines and checklists, that will not only save a parent money but precious time as well by not having to reinvent the wheel. Despite the fact that all children on the spectrum are different, the tips and resources offered can be adjusted to any child's unique needs. The most powerful message that comes across in this book is the importance of planning ahead and providing predictability for a child with autism. The best thing one can do for a child on the spectrum is to create a calm and structured environment, and this book gives the reader the recipe to do just that. The schedules, charts, and routines that are included can make life so much easier for any child on the autism spectrum, and their parents and caregivers as well.

Connie Hammer
MSW & Parent Coach/Consultant
Author of *Autism Parenting: Practical Strategies
for a Positive School Experience*

Ymkje's story is truly the definition of what it means to be an advocate for your child. Her experience of "starting from scratch" with learning about what autism is, and then how to care for an individual on the autism spectrum, is exactly what parents need to hear. She does an excellent job of organizing the puzzle pieces of Logan's story with the appropriate tips, checklists, and tools that are practical, easy to understand, and that will greatly benefit the child and caregiver alike. I would highly recommend this book to anyone who feels overwhelmed, or is looking for where to begin in the world of autism spectrum disorders. Tremendously informative and very well done!

April S. Henry
MA, CCC-SLP

Autism on a Shoestring Budget lets you follow Ms. Wideman-van der Laan's journey as she navigates the many pathways of appropriate accommodations and modifications, and advocates for her grandson Logan as he enters the challenging educational system as a child with autism spectrum and sensory processing disorders. The detailed account of her journey describes the struggles many families go through trying to get the help their child needs in the educational system. She gives excellent advice and needed resources to help parents and caregivers navigate through school systems and life with an ASD child. Ms. Wideman-van der Laan's hands-on life experiences are a valuable resource to those families just starting on this journey of ASD and to those families who need to be pointed in the right direction to get help for their child.

Rebecca Spurgeon
Retired Educator/School Counselor

Autism on a Shoestring Budget is a great guide for new parents who may have children with autism. It is beneficial for teachers to read as well. Often, teachers don't recognize what it is like for parents with autistic children. As someone who has worked in this field for 17+ years, much of the information in this book was familiar to me. However, the section that focused on sensory issues stood out to me, because, in my opinion, I don't think teachers pay enough attention or take into account how serious sensory issues can be for students with autism. I wish teachers would have a stronger background in how to identify sensory issues and, more importantly, how to work with students struggling with sensory issues. This book was a good read. I truly enjoyed it.

Jeremy V. Essen
Special Education Teacher/Mentor

AUTISM ON A
SHOESTRING BUDGET

AUTISM ON A SHOESTRING BUDGET

[Early] Intervention Made Easier

YMKJE WIDEMAN-VAN DER LAAN

ISBN: 9798409116873

Imprint: Independently published

Dedication

To all parents and caregivers who face the daily challenges that come with raising a child on the autism spectrum.

Acknowledgments

I could not have written this book if it were not for Logan, my grandson, whom I had the privilege to care for full-time during the first six years of his life. I continue to be amazed at all he taught me then and continues to teach me as he grows up into a wonderful young man. He is simply amazing. Thank you, Logan. I love you!

I am very grateful to my daughter, Karina, who gave Logan and me a place to live during the early years of caring for him. I could not have stayed in the US without her support and encouragement, and I would never have been exposed to the resources that were made available to me while we lived on the East Coast.

I am also indebted to all the professionals who were involved in my grandson's care during and after his autism diagnosis. The list would be too long if I included the names of everyone who supported and helped Logan during his early years, so I can only mention some of those who were especially involved and contributed in amazing ways:

Rebecca Spurgeon (School Counselor), April Stelly Henry (Speech-Language Pathologist), Therisa Sesvold (Pre-K Teacher), Amy Perry Sparks (Autism Resource Specialist), Dr. Ronald Gibson (School Psychologist), Jamie Kostan (Special Education Lead Teacher), and Jennifer Lingle (Autism Consultant), thank you for helping me see the importance of early and consistent intervention, and for encouraging me every step of the way. Your advice and hands-on, practical involvement made a huge difference in Logan's and my life.

Author's Note

In 2012, when I published my first book, *Autism Is…?*, the Centers for Disease Control (CDC) in the US reported the prevalence of autism as an estimated 1 in 88 children (1 in 54 boys and 1 in 252 girls). Just ten years later, these estimates have risen to a staggering 1 in 44 children, with ASD four times as prevalent among boys as among girls. Whether the rise in these statistics is due to better and earlier detection methods or not, the fact remains that all these children need appropriate intervention—and the earlier the better.

This is, however, often easier said than done, as I found out when my grandson was first diagnosed as autistic in 2010. I knew next to nothing about autism, and when I started to learn what it meant, I felt overwhelmed. I was also stunned at the cost of the recommended therapies and programs that would help my grandson in the present and improve his prospects in the long run. My resources were limited, but I knew I needed to find solutions to provide the best interventions possible. And so I did.

Autism on a Shoestring Budget: [Early] Intervention Made Easier is the story of my autism journey. It includes my personal experiences, as well as material on strategies and interventions that I learned about and was able to implement at little to no cost. I wrote this book because I know firsthand the struggles parents, caregivers, and teachers of autistic children face daily. I hope it will encourage you, and help you find ways to help your unique and awesome child or student with autism too. —Even when on a shoestring budget.

Ymkje Wideman-van der Laan

Contents

The Importance of [Early] Intervention

Dr. Temple Grandin, herself diagnosed with autism at an early age, and many other autism professionals, have spoken extensively on the importance of early intervention and enrolling young children diagnosed with autism in a good educational program as soon as possible.

Dr. Grandin said, "A treatment method or an educational method that will work for one child may not work for another child. The one common denominator for all of the young children is that early intervention does work, and it seems to improve the prognosis."

I have witnessed this personally with my grandson, who was diagnosed with autism spectrum disorder (ASD), sensory processing disorder (SPD), and borderline attention deficit hyperactivity disorder (ADHD) when he was around 3 years old. He hardly spoke, had frequent meltdowns, and self-stimulated by flapping, jumping, and spinning continuously, among other things. Once diagnosed, and thanks to intensive early intervention both in the school setting and at home, he improved rapidly in every area. He became verbally proficient, well-behaved for the most part, and meltdowns became an exception rather than the rule. It was not easy, but all the early, persistent, and consistent hard work paid off.

Some of you reading this may cringe and feel bad that this did not happen for your child for various reasons, and you may wonder if it's too late to start now that your child is older. It's never too late to start, of course, and the results of interventions, even at a later age, can still be phenomenal. However, for those with young children who have just been diagnosed, I can't recommend enough starting as early as possible with an intervention plan.

It is also important to remember that autism is a spectrum disorder. Some children are nonverbal and seem to be severely affected, while others display moderate or mild symptoms, with yet others somewhere in between on the spectrum. Different therapies will work for different children, and there is the reality that no matter how much time, money, and love you put into it, some children may remain nonverbal or not respond the way you hoped they would.

If this is the case in your situation and with your child, please don't be discouraged. All you can do is try your best. Every little intervention helps to some degree in some area of their development, and every little bit of progress is worth your efforts and deserves to be celebrated.

One of your questions may be, as it was for me, "How much is all of this going to cost?" Some good news is that early intervention therapy does not have to be expensive. When I moved to the US and became the full-time caregiver of my grandson, my resources were very limited. I learned through necessity that homemade tools and simple activities can be just as effective as off-the-shelf items and commercial programs when implemented consistently.

You may also wonder where and how to start, as I did when my grandson was first diagnosed. I did not know much about autism and felt overwhelmed by all the information on autism that is available online. Thankfully, the teachers and therapists at my grandson's preschool were extremely helpful in getting me started. Don't hesitate to reach out and ask professionals in your community for suggestions and ideas to help your child.

As you read my story, please remember that interventions should be tailored to each child's unique needs and that the results will vary with each individual. Still, many of the strategies that I will share with you can be tailored to benefit most children on the spectrum. Just use and adapt these suggestions to what you intuitively know your child needs. After all, you know your child best and are your child's best therapist!

CHAPTER 1

The Backstory

It was the first week of October 2006. After attending a long day of meetings in Amman, Jordan, as the regional office manager for a humanitarian organization, I opened my email program and sighed at the sight of a full mailbox. I quickly glanced down the list, looking for anything marked timely or urgent, and abruptly stopped scrolling when I noticed one from my brother-in-law, Clark, in Ohio. Clark rarely emailed me. His message was brief but alarming: Chris needs your help. Call me and I can explain.

Chris, my youngest son, had joined the US Army just before turning 18, and after a recent deployment was stationed at Fort Benning, Georgia. I was very proud of him for completing his Ranger training, getting his wings, and being an exemplary soldier in his unit.

After returning from several tours of duty, he had met a girl in Columbus, Georgia, and after a brief period of dating, they were married. Amanda had a daughter from a previous marriage, whom Chris had accepted wholeheartedly, and they'd welcomed their first child together, a boy, just six months earlier, on April 21, 2006.

They'd seemed happy when I had visited them to help around the time of Logan's birth, but I'd also witnessed some tensions that had concerned me. After I left and went back to work, Chris had called several times. His wife suffered from postpartum depression, he told me. I talked with her and tried to encourage her, but things didn't get better, and from what I could gather from my son's phone calls, he was spending more and more time at home to tend to her and the baby's needs.

After reading Clark's email. I closed my computer and made my way to the upstairs office to place the long-distance call to the States. Clark picked up right away and, in his calm, lawyer-like style, updated me on the situation. Amanda had become so depressed that it had become a safety issue for the baby. She had moved back in with her parents, leaving Chris to care for the baby on his own. "Merrill and Shan have gone down to help Chris take care of Logan," he said, "but they can't stay for long. I think you should come as soon as possible."

I thanked Clark profusely for contacting me right away and assured him that of course I understood that my sister-in-law and niece could not stay to help indefinitely. I told him I'd talk to my supervisor and would try to get there as quickly as I could.

When I later talked to Chris, he confirmed what Clark had shared, and when I told him I could try to come and help for a while, he jumped at the offer. "Could you, Mom? Merrill and Shan are a wonderful help," he said, "but they must go home and get back to work soon. I don't know how I am going to take care of Logan on my own. The army is trying to work with me on this, but it's not been easy." I assured him I'd do my best to come as quickly as I could, and told him to hang in there.

Early the next morning I told my supervisor about the situation, and that I felt I needed to go and help my son—for how long I did not know yet. She was very supportive and told me to start making arrangements. Fortunately, some of my work could be done remotely, so we agreed I would continue to do the best I could while in the States.

The next few weeks were a whirlwind of wrapping up meetings, booking flights, tying up loose ends, and planning for me to continue my work from a distance.

On October 21, 2006, I boarded a flight to Atlanta, Georgia, with my laptop and a small suitcase of belongings I'd packed for what I expected to be a short visit.

CHAPTER 2

Everything Changed

When my plane touched down in Atlanta, I had no idea about the whirlwind of events I was heading into.

Once I had settled in, Merrill updated me on the happenings-to-date, and reluctantly indicated that she and Shan had to prepare for their drive back to Ohio. They were concerned about leaving me alone without transportation while Chris was at work, but I assured them that everything would be all right. They started their drive back home on October 24 and planned to take a few days for the long trip back to Columbus, Ohio.

Before long, I was completely immersed in the care of my six-month-old grandson. Logan was not an easy baby to care for. He cried a lot and had to be carried and rocked to sleep. Once asleep, he would only sleep for short periods at a time and wake easily, and no amount of rocking would get him back to sleep. He also had to be entertained constantly or he would start crying again. The one thing that would quiet him without fail was putting on a DVD with episodes of *Dora the Explorer*. He never seemed to get tired of watching it, and because it was played so often, I soon had the episodes memorized.

In the months that followed, Chris and his wife separated, and because of his incompatible domestic circumstances, there was no other choice than for him to leave the army. After all was said and done, our best option was for Chris, Logan, and me to join my daughter in Jacksonville, North Carolina. She and her husband had recently moved there with my adorable little granddaughter, Ryleigh, who was only ten days younger than Logan.

It was mid-December, 2006, when we made the long drive from Fort Benning to Jacksonville. Chris started looking for work right away and was gone much of the time for interviews. My daughter and I cared for the two 8-month-old cousins, and we soon settled into a daily routine as much as was possible.

Logan continued to be very active and difficult to get to sleep. He also hated driving anywhere in the car and would cry the entire way. He especially screamed when driving after dark. He also preferred to be carried to riding in his stroller, which wasn't always possible considering his rather sturdy frame. It made going anywhere problematic and frustrating, so I often opted to stay home with him rather than tag along on family outings.

As the months passed, during one of his checkups, the pediatrician expressed concern that Logan was not meeting all his milestones, and there were also some other overly active and unusual behaviors he displayed. He said it was too early to tell, but he would not be surprised if Logan were diagnosed with ADHD later in life.

It was true, Logan was never still. He would bounce incessantly in his "stationary" ExerSaucer while watching his still favorite *Dora* episodes on TV, to the point that he made marks across the wooden living room floor. When a visiting family member saw him move across the room like that, she commented that he reminded her of her son at that age, who was diagnosed later with Asperger's syndrome. I had never heard the term before and brushed it off, as surely, he was just a typically healthy and extremely active baby.

Logan's motor development was also different from his same-age cousin, and instead of crawling, as Ryleigh did, he 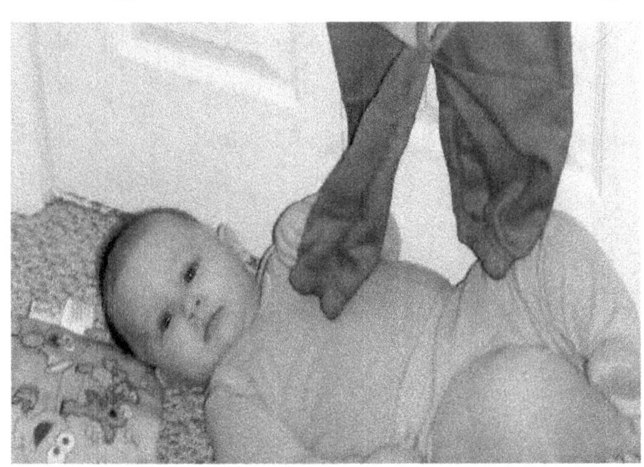 would scoot to something that would catch his eye while lying on his back. He was especially fascinated when a bright piece of clothing would slightly move in the wind of an overhead fan, and fixate on it until able to reach and touch it.

My daughter and I would often comment and laugh at how different Logan and Ryleigh were from each other, but neither of us was too alarmed at that time. Some of his behaviors now stand out as odd, and if I had known anything about autism, I would have been more concerned.

Today, when I look back at photos and watch videos we made of my grandson during his early childhood, I am amazed at how many early autism signs I can detect: He flapped his hands, walked on his tiptoes, engaged in spinning, cried excessively for no apparent reason, made little eye contact, lined up his toys, and it was hard to get his attention.

Of course, all children can occasionally engage in these activities at one time or another, but when they occur often, and for longer periods at a time, these can be red flags for autism.

There are many websites with information on what signs we should most commonly watch out for during early child development. If your child is not meeting these general milestones, or if you are concerned about your child's development, don't wait to consult your pediatrician, because the earlier autism is detected, the better.

10 Early Autism Signs

Here is a list of ten early autism signs to watch for when your child is between 6 and 12 months old:

- Rarely smiles when approached by a parent or caregiver
- Rarely tries to imitate sounds or movements of others
- Engages in delayed or infrequent babbling
- Does not respond to his or her name with increased consistency
- Does not gesture to communicate by 10 months
- Makes poor or no eye contact
- Rarely seeks your attention
- Repeatedly stiffens arms, legs; and/or displays unusual body movements
- Does not reach up toward you when you reach to pick him or her up
- Demonstrates delayed motor development

The American Academy of Pediatrics recommends that all children receive routine developmental screenings, and specific screenings for autism at 9, 18, and 30 months of age.

There are several specialized screening tools to identify children at risk for autism. Most of these screening tools are quick and straightforward, consisting of yes-or-no questions, or a checklist of symptoms. Your pediatrician should also get your feedback regarding your child's behavior.

If your pediatrician detects possible signs of autism during the screening, your child should be referred to a specialist for a comprehensive diagnostic evaluation. Screening tools alone cannot be used to make a diagnosis, which is why further assessment is needed.

The diagnostic process for autism is tricky and can sometimes take a while. But you can take advantage of treatment as soon as the possibility of developmental delays has been confirmed. If this is the case, ask your doctor to refer you to early intervention services.

In the US, early intervention is a federally funded program for infants and toddlers with disabilities. Many studies have shown that around half of children with autism who received early and evidence-based intervention from ages 3 – 5 were able to gain enough skills to be mainstreamed for kindergarten.

Children will benefit from early intervention, even if they do not meet the full criteria for an autism spectrum disorder. In other words, there is more risk involved in the wait-and-see approach than in receiving early intervention.

CHAPTER 3

The Early Years

Shortly after Logan's first birthday, we moved to Auburn, Alabama, where my son had found work. It was there we started noticing some other behaviors that seemed a bit different from "normal." He would excitedly hop up and down in front of the TV while flapping his hands, for example, and walk across the floor on his tiptoes. He was also very slow in starting to speak. On the other hand, he proved to be very bright. Before he was two years old, he could identify word flash cards by pointing after being told a word only once.

When Logan was 2½ years old, we enrolled him in a faith-based, private preschool for several mornings a week. We felt it might help him start speaking more in an environment with other children, and it would also provide me with some much-needed respite.

It wasn't long before I received reports that he often

cried, wanted to be held and rocked a lot, and refused to keep his socks and shoes on. He was simply not behaving like the other two-year-old children in his group. His teacher, Ms. Donna, was so kind and patient with him, but she was also quite concerned, and we were soon encouraged to have Logan evaluated, which we did shortly before his third birthday.

We were relieved to hear that after observation and testing, even though there were some developmental delays, he did not need or qualify for special services.

However, problems in preschool persisted, and we frequently received reports about Logan getting upset, crying, or not participating in activities along with the other children. He had moved up a grade by now, and his new teacher tried her very best to adapt activities to Logan's needs and abilities.

After yet another incident, the preschool director called and asked me to come in. She and several other board members met with me and explained that Logan had melted down while waiting in line, and had put his hands on the child in front of him, squeezing her neck and pushing her. The parents had understandably been very upset because it had scared their daughter.

The director informed me that after discussing it together, they felt that this incident was sufficient reason to expel him and suggested we have Logan retested. They handed me a tuition refund check, and that was it. I left the meeting in tears—upset and sad, and determined to get to the root of these problems.

I contacted local resources and spoke with a child

psychologist shortly afterward. She agreed that retesting him would be the appropriate next step to take, but unfortunately, since the first testing was done so recently, we would have to wait until at least one year had passed.

Luckily, we did not have to wait that long. Some months earlier, my son had found a different and better job with an oil company that worked off the Louisiana coast. My daughter and family had also recently moved there, as her military husband was transferred to Fort Polk.

In June 2010, shortly after Logan's fourth birthday, we made the big move from Alabama to Louisiana to rejoin Logan's dad. Of course, I was thrilled to live near my daughter again, and looked forward to spending time with her and her family.

Looking back on our move there—and the whirlwind of events that followed—fills me with gratitude. If none of that had happened, I would not have found the answers we desperately needed for Logan.

CHAPTER **4**

The Diagnosis

Ve were still in the process of moving into the apartment my son had found in Thibodaux, Louisiana, when we found out that due to the effects of the Deepwater Horizon oil spill, the largest marine oil spill in history, caused by an April 2010 explosion on the Deepwater Horizon oil rig—approximately 41 miles (66 km) off the coast of Louisiana—my son lost his newly acquired job.

Thankfully, he found employment and was rehired by an oil company in California shortly afterward, but that meant he had to move to the West Coast almost immediately. After talking it over together with my daughter and her husband, we all felt it best for Logan and me to temporarily move in with them again, since they had the room. It would also make it possible for Logan to go to the same school as his cousin Ryleigh. So just a few days later we moved to Fort Polk.

The next few months were very busy. There was so much

to be done: registering address changes, working out the needed paperwork for me to act as Logan's legal guardian while my son worked out of state, finding a pediatrician for Logan, updating vaccinations to match the state requirements, registering him for preschool, and so much more.

While enrolling Logan for the Head Start program that operated in one of the Fort Polk elementary schools, I explained some of the problems we had encountered in Logan's previous private preschool and I requested a class with an experienced teacher who would be patient and understanding of him. I was so relieved when my request was respectfully acknowledged and noted.

Logan and I were able to meet with Mrs. Therisa before school started, and I was encouraged by her positive attitude and reassuring approach. We instantly connected and developed an open channel of communication from day one, lasting throughout the year that followed.

Logan's first day of preschool was on September 7, 2010. It did not take long before Mrs. Therisa and others noticed that Logan was different. A meeting was scheduled with Mrs. Spurgeon, the school counselor, who had just started her last year in this position before retirement. I had Logan with me when we met, and he quietly played with some blocks in a small play area set up in a corner of her office. I passed on his previous evaluation to her and explained what had happened in the private preschool.

After watching Logan play and interact with her, she told me that she suspected Logan may be autistic and suggested having him retested right away. She explained that under Louisiana state laws, Logan would qualify for services, and she assured me they were going to do their very best for him—and so they did.

Even before his reevaluation was completed, he started daily special classes along with weekly speech and occupational therapy immediately, while remaining in his mainstream classroom with his wonderful and patient teacher for the rest of the day.

On January 14, 2011, I received and signed the test results. Logan's diagnosis included "classic high-functioning" autism spectrum disorder, sensory processing disorder, and borderline attention deficit hyperactivity disorder.

While this came as no surprise, it was now official. In many ways, I felt relieved to have a name for the challenging behaviors we had faced for quite some time already, but the relief was not the only feeling I experienced. In the weeks and months that followed, I went from sad to being angry, from frustrated to feeling baffled and overwhelmed about what to do next, to name just a few emotions.

As a single grandmother, and at that time sole caregiver of my grandson, the challenges loomed very big. I was struggling financially and felt stretched in every direction to keep up with working remotely while also taking care of Logan.

I was so lucky to have the encouragement of my daughter, as well as supporting school staff to help me through the initial months after the diagnosis. Thanks to their input, I soon realized that indulging in negative emotions would not have a positive effect on my grandson, or anyone else for that matter. I had to pull myself together!

When I started focusing on all the possibilities rather than the things my grandson may never be able to do, I started seeing amazing progress. Whenever I followed the directions of his teachers and therapists with high expectations and did my best to reinforce them consistently at home, he met those expectations almost without fail.

Accepting the news of an autism diagnosis takes time, and everyone processes the news of a diagnosis differently and in their own time. Some adjust quickly, and others may take longer, which of course is perfectly fine. There were ups and downs and moments of despair, but as I started to accept Logan's autism, it became easier to handle the challenges.

A child on the autism spectrum experiences the world differently, and I slowly began to better understand his perspective, which enabled me to help Logan navigate through his largely neurotypical environment. It took time to learn that I needed to try to see the world through his eyes—and I'm still learning.

The Grieving Process

Everyone experiences the news that "Your child has autism" differently, and everyone reacts differently.

The reactions can range from "I knew it! I have been telling the doctors this for the last twelve months," and "I don't think it is autism," to "Really? I think he is just getting a slow start."

Many families go through a process very similar to the grieving process: They mourn the loss of the hopes and dreams they had for their child.

There are usually five stages of grief:

- **Denial:** "I can't believe this is happening!"
- **Anger:** "I am so hurt and angry this is happening to my child!"
- **Bargaining:** For autism parents, this could be listed as hope: "If I enroll in every possible therapy, maybe the autism will disappear."
- **Depression:** "I am heartbroken and feel so hopeless about my child's future."
- **Acceptance:** "I am ready to take the next steps. What do I need to do to help my child? I am going to be okay. My child is going to be okay."

Grief isn't one-size-fits-all. It takes time to go through each stage of the grieving process, which will be different for everyone, and these stages may recur, or happen in no particular order. Even after many years, parents can experience waves of sadness and depression, as reflected in the despairing comment by a dad of an autistic 13-year-old: "All I wanted was a normal son."

It's very important to remember that everyone experiences grief differently. There is no specific way to feel grief. You may experience feelings of grief much more intensely than the other parent or family members, or you may seem unaffected while others around you are struggling to get through it.

Whatever the case, allow yourself time to feel and adjust to an autism diagnosis, and seek help and support if needed.

CHAPTER 5

So Much to Learn!

After Mrs. Spurgeon told me about the possibility of autism, I wanted to learn all I could about it, as I was completely unfamiliar with what it was and what it meant. Looking for information was overwhelming, so I was very thankful for Logan's first speech-language pathologist (SLP), Mrs. April Henry, who helped me get started by making recommendations.

The first thing I watched was the then newly released HBO movie, *Temple Grandin*. In the movie, before enrolling in college, famed animal husbandry expert Temple Grandin (Claire Danes) visits a cattle ranch owned by her aunt Ann (Catherine O'Hara) and demonstrates a brilliance for all things mechanical. Once classes begin, the autistic Grandin rises to meet the intellectual challenges—although the social ones were more difficult. Grandin ultimately triumphs over prejudice to become an innovator in the field of animal care.

Today, Mary Temple Grandin (born August 29, 1947), is an American professor of animal science at Colorado State University, a consultant to the livestock industry on animal behavior, and an autism spokesperson. She was one of the first individuals on the autism spectrum to publicly share insights from her personal experience of autism.

This film had a profound effect on me and moved me to tears. At the end of it, after watching the final scene where Temple talks about the difference her mother made in her life, I made a conscious commitment to be to Logan what Temple's mother was to her.

The book *There's a Boy in Here* (by Judy Barron and Sean Barron) also moved me deeply. It helped to put into perspective some of the challenges that l could expect to face and prepared me at least somewhat for those challenges, but also instilled hope that with persistence and patience, I would be able to see Logan reach his full potential.

After that, I read everything I could find on the subject. I subscribed to blogs and websites, and I worked closely with Logan's regular and special education teachers, his speech-language pathologist, and his occupational therapist (OT). There was so much to learn.

Over time, more and more pieces of the puzzle started to fit together, and many of the unspoken questions I'd had for some time were getting answered one by one.

What Is Autism?

Autism spectrum disorder (ASD) is a neurological (brain) disorder that affects communication, social interaction, and behavior.

Individuals with autism typically have difficulty understanding verbal and/or nonverbal communication, and learning appropriate ways of relating to other people, objects, and events. Dr. Temple Grandin once noted, "I think autistic brains tend to be specialized brains. Autistic people tend to be less social. It takes up a ton of processor space in the brain to have all the social circuits."

As its name implies, ASD is a "spectrum" disorder that affects individuals differently and with varying degrees of severity. No two people with ASD are the same. Dr. Stephen Shore famously said, "If you have met one person with autism, you have met one person with autism." He explained, "This quote emphasizes that there is great diversity within the autism spectrum. While the commonalities of people on the autism spectrum include differences in communication, social interaction, sensory receptivity, and highly focused interests, it's important to understand that the constellation of these characteristics blends differently for everyone. This is why some on the spectrum are good at mathematics while others may be good in arts, sports, or writing—just like the rest of humanity. Autism is an extension of the diversity found in the human gene pool."

How common is autism?

Autism is more common than childhood cancer, cystic fibrosis, and multiple sclerosis combined. According to the Centers for Disease Control (CDC), in the US alone, 1 out of every 44 children born today has some form of ASD.

Based on statistics from the US Department of Education and others, autism is growing at a startling rate of 10–17 percent per year. It is estimated to be on average 4 times more likely to occur in boys than in girls.

Autism knows no boundaries of race, ethnicity, social status, family income, lifestyle, or educational levels, and can affect any family and any child.

What causes autism?

We know that there's no one cause of autism. Research suggests that autism develops from a combination of genetic and nongenetic, or environmental, influences.

CHAPTER 6

Sensory Issues—
It Finally Made Sense

When discussing some of my grandson's most challenging behaviors after learning that autism might be a possibility, his therapists told me that most, if not all of them, could be rooted in sensory deficits.

When Logan was diagnosed with SPD, I was so happy to finally understand the cause of his inconsolable crying when I put on his socks and shoes, his resistance to tooth and hair brushing, and a host of other sensory-related upsets. It finally made sense.

Excessive crying while riding in the car, getting upset at loud sounds, not being able to handle and melting down in crowds or rooms with bright lights, were just a few of the things I had been dealing with for quite some time and occurred on an almost daily basis.

Putting on socks and shoes especially had been a major

ordeal for as long as I could remember. As soon as I put them on, he'd start crying and take them off again. It especially was a problem when going out. The minute he got in the car, his socks and shoes were on the floor.

I learned from his occupational therapist who diagnosed his sensory processing disorder that putting on those regular socks with seams might feel to him what it feels like to us when we have a small, sharp rock in our shoe. No wonder he cried!

I was grateful to learn that I could relieve the discomfort he experienced by taking simple steps to start helping him.

As Logan was extremely sensitive to the touch of other textures too, she showed me a

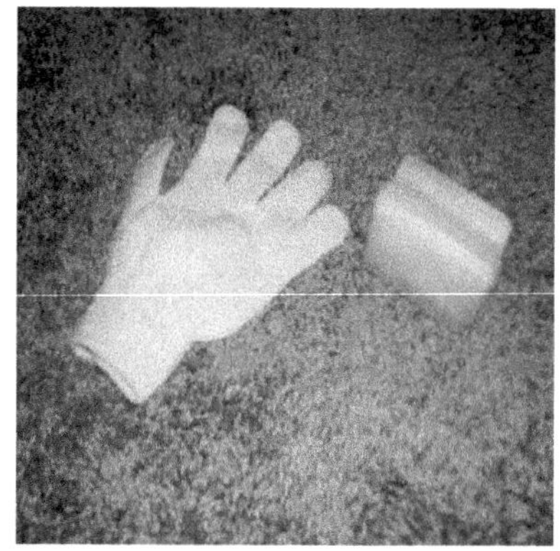

desensitizing brushing routine, gave me a list of exercises I could do with him at home that would help regulate his over-responsiveness to touch, and she also recommended I buy him comfortable, soft clothes, seamless socks, and more comfortable shoes with Velcro closing.

I found those seamless socks and more comfortable shoes and pants, and cut tags out of shirts as soon as I brought them home from the store. I also started carrying a set of noise-dampening headphones with me to use when sounds in certain places were too loud and upsetting for him.

Over time, with consistent brushing, doing the recommended exercises, and gentle exposure to sensory input, his sensitivities began to improve. These may seem like very small "victories" to some, but seeing my grandson get dressed without melting down and better able to endure the overwhelming sensory input in public places like shopping centers, grocery stores, public bathrooms, and restaurants was a huge relief and extremely rewarding. Taking positive action paid off!

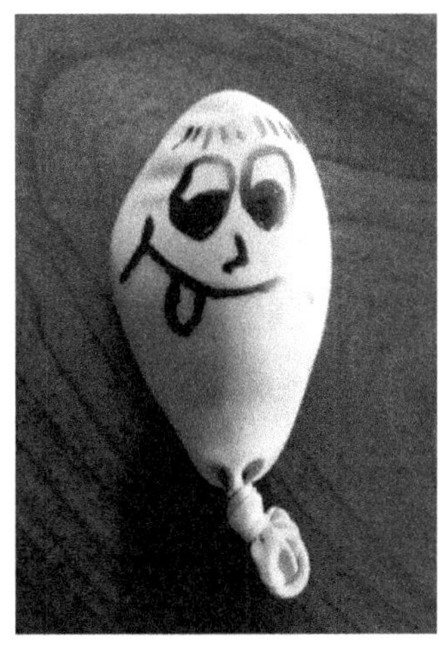

While in preschool, Logan's struggles with various sensory issues also often interfered with his ability to concentrate or focus on the activities at hand. When his teacher had a hard time redirecting or distracting him from these sensory discomforts, Mrs. Henry had the brilliant idea of creating a fidget toy out of a balloon! She filled the deflated balloon partly with flour, tied a knot in it, and then drew a cute little face on it with a permanent marker!

Of course, fidget toys are available in all sorts of shapes, sizes, textures, and colors, and they can range in price from cheap to expensive, but this may very well be the easiest to make and cheapest gadget ever! This was Logan's favorite fidget toy for a long time, and holding and squeezing his Silly Balloon never failed to bring a smile to his face.

While these and other early interventions helped Logan to become more sensory tolerant over the years, that does not mean he does not have SPD anymore. Even today, at age 15, something may bother him that hasn't affected him for a great while. His socks, no longer seamless, may start upsetting him after becoming scratchy inside after many washes. The feel of something he has touched many times may suddenly turn him off, or the sight, sound, or smell of something that hasn't bothered him may unexpectedly be intolerable. As a teenager, he recently developed an aversion to the color yellow, and sometimes seeing yellow food, like his previously favorite Mac 'n' Cheese, can make him feel physically sick to his stomach, and even result in a meltdown.

When things like this happen, it can be easy for some to minimize it or not make the connection between SPD and the ensuing meltdown right away. This is why it is important to educate others and remind them that SPD is a neurological disorder that will never really go away. Consistent intervention does help children with SPD to become more sensory tolerant, but there are times when something may suddenly bother them again.

It is also important to remember that a child with SPD can experience pain or become physically ill from certain sensory inputs, which, if felt by anyone else at that level, would trigger a reaction, too.

The sooner we can work with our children and teach them how to address any sensory issues appropriately the better. If verbal, they can learn to use their words to express what they are feeling and ask for help instead of melting down uncontrollably, which can upset those around them and leave people baffled as to what triggered the sudden breakdown. If nonverbal, it is important to try to find another way for them to express their discomfort, so they can respond accordingly and appropriately. Having visual supports—pictures a non- or less-verbal child can point to—can be very helpful.

Visual supports can also help manage certain sensitivities.

During Logan's preschool years, loud noises would often startle him, especially unexpected automatic toilet flushes in public restrooms. This was quite a problem at times, especially when we had to go out shopping. I always made sure that he went to the bathroom before we went out and tried to keep our trips short, but there were still times we were out longer. It was nearly impossible to get him to enter a public restroom at those times. He'd just freeze outside the door with his hands covering his ears, screaming "Noooo!" at the top of his voice.

At home, Logan had an orange betta fish, which he named Lasagna, after his favorite "orange" food! He loved coming home and sitting in front of Lasagna's small fish tank. Watching him swim around had a tremendous calming effect on him.

I told Mrs. Henry, his SLP, about this, and about his fear of restrooms. She had the idea to use his special bond with Lasagna to address his bathroom fears and found a picture of an orange betta fish online. On the back of the picture card she wrote, "Lasagna the fish is very brave. He swims all alone in his tank and braves the loud noises around him. He stays calm when he hears a loud sound and just keeps swimming. Just like me. I'll keep doing what I need to do when I hear loud noises. I am brave just like Lasagna."

I would read and show him the card before we went out, and talk with him about being brave like Lasagna in case he needed to use the restroom. This power card worked wonders and helped him overcome his fears the very first time we used it when he had to go to the bathroom while out. That little card went with us everywhere for a long time, until he learned to manage without it.

Showing your child that you respect his feelings, acknowledging his discomfort, and finding a solution to the problem together will minimize the trauma that often accompanies sensory issues, and will eventually help your child learn to cope with them independently.

If your child has sensory issues, I hope you can find the reasons, and get helpful advice on how to minimize the causes, and gently and persistently desensitize your child. It will make a huge difference, as it did for Logan.

What Is Sensory Processing Disorder?

Sensory processing disorder (SPD) is a neurological disorder that causes difficulties with taking in, processing, and responding to sensory information about the environment and from within an individual's own body.

The senses include visual, auditory, tactile, olfactory (smell), gustatory (taste), vestibular (balance and spatial orientation), and kinesthetic (the sense of one's limbs in space).

A child with SPD is either going to act out or withdraw to manage the overwhelming stimuli of their environment. Some 80% of individuals with autism also have SPD.

What are the symptoms?

Behavioral: Withdrawal from touch; difficulty calming oneself; refusing certain foods; hypersensitivity to fabrics and tags; disliking dirt; avoiding creative play; repetitive play or TV watching; oversensitivity to sound, odors, and background noises; accidentally harming others; dangerous behaviors.

Physical: Odd posture; poor balance; delayed fine and gross motor skills; impaired sleep, eating, and elimination patterns; constant motion; jumping; poor coordination; high or low pain tolerance.

Psychosocial: Anxiety; depression; social isolation; fear of crowds and sudden touch; standing too close to others.

How can we help?

Adapt clothing: Provide seamless socks, soft clothing without tags or with tags cut out, soft shoes with Velcro closing, etc.

Adapt lighting: Many autistic children have difficulty in rooms with fluorescent lights. Provide lamps with incandescent light bulbs, if possible.

Adapt surroundings: Overstimulating environments can result in sensory overload and meltdowns. Use less stimulating décor in bedrooms and classrooms. Fish tanks can have a calming effect.

Adapt noise level: Provide noise-dampening headphones when needed for outings and assemblies. Tabletop water fountains at home or in the classroom can have a calming effect.

Provide appropriate exercises: Shoulder presses, wall push-ups, and jumping on a small trampoline can be helpful. Consult an Occupational Therapist, if possible, for exercises tailored to your child's needs.

Provide sensory gadgets and chew toys: Fidget toys are available in all sorts of shapes, sizes, textures, and colors, and they can range in price from cheap to expensive.

I have been talking and writing about sensory problems for over 20 years, and am still perplexed by many people who do not acknowledge sensory issues and the pain and discomfort they can cause.

A person doesn't have to be on the autism spectrum
to be affected by sensory issues.

Dr. Temple Grandin
Author of *The Way I See It*

CHAPTER 7

Meltdowns

Once Logan started preschool at North Polk Elementary, and long before his "official" diagnosis, it became obvious that he would need significant accommodations to be successful in his mainstream classroom. I will be forever grateful to his preschool teacher and SLP for their support and patience with me as I learned about strategies and interventions that might help Logan.

Logan often had meltdowns, which prompted his teachers, Mrs. Therisa and Mrs. Henry, to ask me for a list of what I thought triggered Logan to get upset. The list I compiled after reflecting on Logan's meltdowns at home or while out was the beginning of regular communication with Logan's school team. I would email updates, questions, and concerns, and they would answer my questions whenever we met formally in meetings, or informally when I dropped off or picked Logan up from school.

Here is the list I sent to Logan's team in November 2010 of things that seemed to trigger his meltdowns the most:

Changes in routine:

- Changing plans at the last minute, like going to a different store than originally planned. I try to avoid this as much as possible.

- Not doing something in the set ritual he is already used to, such as his bedtime routine. If he forgets to say goodnight to his betta fish, Lasagna, for example, he will cry in bed until he can "start over" and I let him get up to say goodnight to his pet. He will go to sleep without a problem after that.

Other things that upset him:

- Certain foods mixing on his plate. He likes his sectional plate, and it must be in front of him a certain way, or he will turn it.

- Me inadvertently taking a bite of his food to taste it or see if it is too hot before giving him his served plate or snack. He will want me to start serving his plate all over again.

- Missing a landmark that he watched for on his way to or from school or the store. He will want to go back and "start over" so he can see the street sign again, for example.

- Me not understanding something he wants, and giving him the wrong item.

- Some loud noises, such as the vacuum cleaner. He

will sit on the couch or bed with his feet drawn up until I turn it off.

- A change in who is at the car line in the morning. He prefers Ms. Pagan to take him out of the car, and on a bad day refuses anyone else. On a good day, he will go with others, but even then, it takes preparing him once I see Ms. Pagan is not there. I try and make a big deal when I see one of the other assistants. For example, "Look, Logan, we've got Ms. Maria today!" Now when we drive up, he will say, "Who do we got?"

- Standing in line is something he dislikes very much, and he will try to run away if he can.

- Ending an activity, or transitioning from one thing to another. We had a big problem with this recently when they were offering children's games at a community center. He wanted to keep bowling, but there were people behind us waiting for their turn, so he had to move on. It ended up creating a big scene in public, with uncle having to carry him back to the car.

- When he puts a sticker on his chart and it breaks or goes on crooked, he gets pretty upset. Things do break sometimes, but it usually helps if I can "fix" it and assure him that it's no big deal, or if I give him a new sticker.

I would appreciate any tips you may have for me, especially on how to handle meltdowns in public as gracefully as possible. He tends to throw himself on the floor, and since he is so big, it is very hard for me to lift him. Thankfully, most of the time he does okay, especially when I prepare him for what is planned, but he does have unexplained very "bad days" when out in the community. It has resulted in critical comments from bystanders at times, which can be embarrassing and upsetting.

This first communication prompted a meeting with Mrs. Henry, Logan's SLP, who introduced me to the concept and importance of using visual supports. All this was new to me, but she made it so simple and easy to implement that I still use her method to this day with other autistic students I teach.

She made a set of cards addressing some of the issues I had listed, using construction paper and pictures from magazines, which she laminated and put on a keyring. *Logan's Key Chain Rules* included the following problem areas:

- **Mistake Rule:** Making mistakes is okay, they can be fixed.
- **Patience Rule:** Having patience when in line or taking turns.
- **Food Rule:** Asking for help when foods touch or mix.
- **Danger Rule:** Listening when warned of danger.

She explained that reviewing simply-worded stories and illustrated rules regularly before problem behavior occurs can often help prevent meltdowns. It usually does not work to read the rules just before or during a meltdown or potentially volatile situation, she said, as the child is already upset and losing control. She also made two sets of everything—one to keep at school to be used by the teacher, and one for me to keep and use at home. That way we would all use the same strategies and interventions when Logan needed extra support with sudden changes and transitions or when he got upset over other things.

Using these simple visual tools consistently was very effective, and after some time Logan's meltdowns decreased significantly as he learned to cope better with situations that upset him.

I also learned that engaging with a child in meltdown mode and trying to stop him verbally or physically from being upset is rarely effective. It's not always easy to stay calm and collected when a child is acting out, but trying to put ourselves in his shoes, acknowledging, and even joining him in the frustration that caused the breakdown in the first place might just be the thing that helps turn the tide.

I will never forget an example of this while picking him up from his classroom one day.

Logan had been in his special education class just before it was time to go home. He usually would be excited to see me and ready to go, but not that day. He was on the floor in front of his mainstream classroom door, crying inconsolably. At age 4, Logan's verbal communication skills were still minimal and the expressions of his wants and needs were generally limited to one or two words or pointing to an object. In-between his sobs and his pointing down the hallway, all we could make out was the word "video," which didn't make much sense.

It was then that Mrs. Therisa decided to lie down beside him on the floor in the school hallway. She quietly joined him in his grief and sympathized. I watched in amazement as Logan calmed down and pointed down the hall toward his special education classroom.  She told him, "Okay, let's go there and look." He led her to a shelf with Winnie the Pooh videos, which at that time were his absolute favorite. He'd found one that we didn't have at home yet, and had watched a little of it in his special class before it was time to go home.

His special education teacher graciously let him borrow the video that day, and I went home with a firsthand example of compassion in action.

We later worked with Logan on communicating his needs in more appropriate ways, but I learned that day that showing a child that we sympathize and are trying to understand his distress goes a lot further than engaging in a verbal or physical battle to stop a meltdown. Thank you, Mrs. Therisa.

Tips for Prevention, Intervention, and Postvention

Prevention Strategy

- Show and read visual stories or rules of appropriate behavior when the child is calm.
- Review these stories and rules consistently every day or several times a day before a specific behavior occurs.
- Don't read the rules to the child in front of an audience if it will embarrass the child.
- Refer to the stories or rules positively and praise the child when they demonstrate acceptable behavior.

Intervention Strategy

- Refer to the visual support by pointing or tapping on it at the beginning of escalating behavior.
- Talk low, talk slow, don't say much, or say nothing at all! Stay very calm.

Postvention Strategy

- Reference and review the rules after the crisis is over. This depersonalizes the situation.
- Ensure the child is in a therapeutic state and is calm before talking about the rules or story. Premature referencing may cause the behavior to escalate again.

CHAPTER 8

Public Meltdowns

If you have ever had your child lie on the ground in the middle of a supermarket with his ears covered and screaming at the top of his lungs, you know that it can be extremely embarrassing and difficult to handle—especially when bystanders stare, frown, or make judgmental comments like, "If that was my child, he'd get a good swift kick in the pants!"

When Logan was 4 and 5 years old, public meltdowns were frequent occurrences, and I struggled with how to handle those gracefully. I often felt embarrassed, defensive, desperate, heartbroken, and upset all at the same time. When I confided to Mrs. Henry about this, she was not only sympathetic and encouraging, but she also gave me the perfect way to handle situations like this.

She explained that meltdowns in supermarkets or restaurants are often due to sensory overload. The lights, sounds, and smells may just be too much for an autistic child to process. If possible, it's always best to try to remove the child from the situation. But when this is not possible, she agreed that in the throes of trying to calm down a distraught child is hardly the time for verbal explanations or promoting autism awareness to bystanders. The next time I saw her she had printed out a batch of small cards for me that she found on the website of the University of Indiana. The text read:

This Child Has Autism

You may have seen behavior that seems unusual. If so, it is because this child has an autism spectrum disorder (ASD). ASDs are neurological disorders that affect 1 out of 150 people.* Children with ASDs have difficulty understanding how to act in social settings and communicate their needs. Because this child has an ASD, this child must be taught many things that most people learn naturally. We are helping this child learn by teaching appropriate ways to react and interact. Please help us by being respectful and understanding of this child's special needs.

I couldn't have been more grateful for this. Handing this card with a kind smile to an especially questioning or commenting individual never failed to get an apology, and sometimes even some help when needed and appropriate.

---

* In December 2021, the CDC released new data indicating the prevalence of autism is now 1 in 44 children.

Even though I do not have to use these anymore, I still have a small supply on hand just in case I meet a parent or caregiver in one of my workshops who may need and appreciate them as much as I did then.

CHAPTER 9

Transitions and Changes

It was obvious from the examples that I had reported, as well as from what was happening at school, that Logan had difficulty handling sudden change and transitioning from one activity to another. After reading my list, Mrs. Henry proceeded to make several "storybooks" for Logan addressing change and sudden changes. She showed me that making this kind of storybook and any kind of visual support does not have to be expensive or difficult but can be cheap and easy.

She simply folded a piece of colorful construction paper in half, wrote or drew a short story addressing a behavior, and added pictures cut from magazines to illustrate it.

Over time, I collected quite a few of these stories, and to keep them all in one place and easily accessible, I created Logan's Toolbox! I found a plastic container with an attached lid, which Logan had a blast decorating with shiny animal stickers. We then placed all his visual tools and sensory gadgets inside of it and added any new ones to it as needed. That box went with us everywhere for years.

One way to help Logan transition during his school day was Logan's Schedule Stick that Mrs. Henry made for him. Again, it was a cheap and easy solution for a big need.

She glued a strip of Velcro onto a wooden ruler, printed out

and laminated small event cards, and glued a Velcro dot to the back of the cards to attach to the ruler in order of events. I would attach the cards to the stick before my grandson left for school, and once he was in the classroom, he'd remove the first card (follow the footprints) and put it in a plastic baggie on his desk. All through the day, he would remove the labels from the stick until the last one was gone and it was time for me to pick him up.

It became part of Logan's morning routine to carry his schedule stick on his way to school, which also helped to keep his little hands busy and his focus on carrying it and standing in line to walk into the school building instead of eloping once out of the car. It worked like a charm most of the time. Creating this visual schedule did not cost more than a couple of dollars, and served a great purpose until it was replaced by a different type.

As Logan learned to read, I started writing out his daily schedule with him each morning after breakfast and before going to school, which remained a ritual for several years.

This helped to prepare him for transitioning from one activity to another during his preschool hours. If there were any foreseen changes in the schedule, Mrs. Therisa would let me know ahead of time as much as possible, so I could include it in his written schedule and prepare him accordingly. I would talk about his schedule while writing it down, and after a while, he started to carry this list to school in place of his schedule stick. At school, he would cross off each event as it happened.

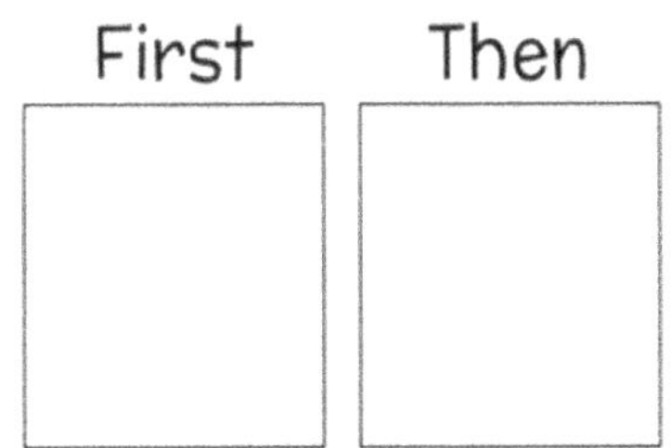

Another visual tool that I used often with Logan, and still use occasionally, was a First/Then chart. I created one in a Word document, printed and laminated it, and had it available in different sizes along with a supply of dry erase markers. There was always one handy somewhere—on the counter in the kitchen, in Logan's bedroom, in the car, in my purse, and on his desk at school.

As Logan learned to read, the stick figures I used initially when he was much younger gave way to written words on his First/Then chart. I used it to help him transition from one activity to another, remind him to calm down when in meltdown mode so we could "then" go on to a preferred activity, tell him about a fun surprise he would get to do after his chores, give him instructions for early morning wake-ups, and more.

I'd simply say, "Logan, look!" while holding up the First/Then chart. He'd stop to read it, which helped him focus, and sometimes he read the instruction aloud. More often than not, he'd follow through without any issues on the directions I'd written down on his chart.

Of course, each unique child with autism will react differently. Still, this simple visual tool is great to have on hand. As a bonus, the back of it can be used as a little drawing board while out in the car or in waiting rooms. Wipe it clean with an eraser, paper towel, or tissue, and it's ready to use again.

Visual Supports and Why We Use Them

Visual support refers to using a picture or other visual item to communicate with a child who has difficulty understanding or using language. Visual supports can be photographs, drawings, objects, written words, or lists. Research has shown that visual supports work well to communicate.

Visual supports are used with children who have autism spectrum disorders for two main purposes. They help parents communicate better with their children, and they help their children communicate better with others.

Visual supports can be used with persons of any age. Also, visual supports can be used by caregivers other than parents.

Why are visual supports important?

The main features of ASD are challenges in interacting socially, using language, and having limited interests or repetitive behaviors. Visual supports help in all three areas.

First, children with ASD may not understand social cues as they interact with others in daily activities. They may not grasp social expectations, like how to start a conversation, how to respond when others make social approaches, or how to change behavior based on unspoken social rules. Visual supports can help teach social skills and help children with ASD use them on their own in social situations.

Second, children with ASD often find it difficult to understand and follow spoken instructions. They may not be able to express well what they want or need. Visuals can help parents communicate what they expect. This decreases frustration and may help decrease problem behaviors that result from difficulty communicating. Visuals can promote appropriate, positive ways to communicate.

Finally, some children with ASD are anxious or act out when their routines change or they are in unfamiliar situations. Visuals can help them understand what to expect and what will happen next and reduce anxiety. Visuals can help them pay attention to important details and help them cope with change.

Written by Whitney Loring, PsyD, TRIAD Postdoctoral Fellow, and Mary Hamilton, MEd, BCBA, TRIAD Educational and Behavioral Consultant.

CHAPTER **10**

Taking Trips Together

In November 2010, just after the start of Logan's 2010–2011 preschool year, we moved into an apartment right outside of Fort Polk. Living off-post, but still close to my daughter and her family was an adjustment, but Logan settled in well. He loved his new room, and the cul-de-sac and nearby playground provided a safe area for him to run and play to his heart's content.

His dad visited whenever he could, of course, and his visits were highlights for both of us. It would give me a little reprieve and a much-needed break from being the sole caregiver, and Logan loved the extra attention, too.

My sister also came for a visit from the Netherlands in March 2011. Logan loved his great-aunt and had a lot of fun working on school projects with her. Our spring break trip to New Orleans together with my sister and my daughter's family was a great experience for him—and me as well.

We'd taken a road trip with my daughter's family to the Houston Zoo during the summer of 2010, and it had been a bit of a rough ride at that time. Logan melted down several times  during that trip, which had gotten everyone upset and resulted in some very tense moments. He did enjoy his time at the zoo, even though it was extremely hot that summer, and despite the challenges, we ended up with some happy memories to look back on.

However, the challenges we faced on that trip made me wonder how he would do on this second road trip, and I was more than a little apprehensive as to how he would react to the long ride in the back of the full van. He and his same-age cousin, Ryleigh, would be seated in the very back with me in between them, my sister and baby Raiden in the middle row, and my daughter and her husband up-front.

Thankfully, the van was equipped with a DVD player, and my son-in-law had attached two video monitors to the backs of the middle seats, so Logan and Ryleigh were entertained most of the time while traveling. To my relief, there hardly were any issues, and he was quite happy both ways.

I was also a bit worried about how he would react to staying in a hotel and sleeping in a different bed. His routine would be pretty much out of the window, and everything would be new and different from what he was used to at home. I tried to prepare him by letting him know how long the trip would be; showing him pictures of the hotel we'd stay in; and talking about the fun things we would do, but only time would tell how he'd react, of course.

Looking back now, I realize I should not have worried as much, because while Logan kept me and my sister hopping during this trip, I was happily surprised at how well he reacted and adjusted. He loved having this time with his cousin, and though he parallel played most of the time and did not always have the same interests as she did, it ended up being a great trip for everyone.

His favorite part of the trip was our visit to New Orleans's Audubon Aquarium of the Americas. Logan loved watching the fish and even got to touch some of them.

He loved the otters best. He would walk with them as they swam from one side of the big tank to the other, and to this day I am convinced he communicated with them. He would stop, and they would stop and look at him. He'd walk again and they'd start swimming again. He had laughing-out-loud fun with this, and when it was time to leave, we had a hard time getting him away from the otter tank.

CHAPTER 11

Summer Vacation

Toward the end of the school year, with summer vacation about to start, I realized I needed some input for the summer months we would be spending at home together.

Summer vacation is a big change for any child, but for a child with autism, the variation from his daily routine can be especially upsetting. It can also be a challenge for parents and caregivers, as they will have to come up with and introduce a new daily schedule, and provide meaningful and engaging activities for several months.

Preparing ahead of time is always best, of course. This may come naturally and easily to some, but for others, it may be a daunting assignment. Circumstances are a factor too. There may be other siblings in the equation, finances are tighter for some than for others, there's work to be done, both at home and in the workplace, and the list goes on.

For me, keeping things simple and functional helps me

to avoid that overwhelming feeling that tends to paralyze me when there just seems to be too much to do. I also like to use checklists. It feels great to check off those boxes, even if it's just one or two at a time. It gives me a feeling of accomplishment, and that even if not everything is done, at least I've done something.

I made the following checklist to prepare for our summer vacation. Of course, it can be adapted and added to as needed, as each family and child's needs are unique, but perhaps it can serve as a good idea or starting point.

I also asked Logan's teachers and therapists for assignments and goals that Logan could work on, and they were so helpful.

My Summer Checklist

Things to ask the teacher:

- ☐ Three assignments/goals that would be good to work on during the summer months
- ☐ Any leftover extra worksheets or workbooks that could be sent home
- ☐ Any tips/strategies to use at home that worked well at school
- ☐ Recommendations for summer programs and activities in the area
- ☐ Email addresses or phone numbers of the parents of children in the class to set up playdates

Things to do to prepare me:

- ☐ Collect ideas for arts and crafts and put the needed materials in a box for easy access
- ☐ Prepare outside activity gear and make it easily accessible; i.e., swimming gear, baseball glove, balls, bike gear, Frisbees, etc.
- ☐ Organize school assignments, worksheets, and books
- ☐ Make a list of possible outings/activities to keep on hand, including locations and admission costs, and pencil in outing dates on the calendar
- ☐ Prepare a reading list or a box of books to read during the summer months. Keep a reading log.

- [ ] Have a reward box with small prizes to encourage completing assignments or reaching goals. Dollar stores are a great resource!

- [ ] Draw up a list of fun activities to do together. This can include gardening, making a bird feeder, cooking, or baking, swimming lessons, visiting someone, etc.

Things to do to prepare my child:

- [ ] Talk about and/or write a social story about summer vacation and the last day of school

- [ ] Prepare a new daily visual schedule for the summer days. (Remember to schedule outside activities during the coolest part of the day.)

- [ ] Talk about and/or make a social story about set activities and surprise activities that will happen during summer

- [ ] If vacation or a trip is planned, mark it on the calendar, talk about and/or make a social story with pictures of what will happen and where we will be going

- [ ] Ask my child for his/her ideas and wishes, too, and include their requests in the planning as much as possible.

CHAPTER 12

Moving

Just before the start of summer vacation, my daughter's husband found out that he would be transferred to Fort Bragg in North Carolina. After talking it over, we all felt it best for me to move with them, so we arranged for a large moving truck for our combined belongings. The house on-post they would be moving into would not be large enough to fit all of us, so I would need to look for an off-post apartment for Logan and me immediately upon arrival.

Needless to say, this meant yet an additional change for Logan, so I set out to prepare him the best I could with visual and verbal stories about our move.

My main concern was the very long drive we'd be taking together in the van with my daughter and her now two children, Ryleigh and baby Raiden, who was born on April 1, 2010. We'd be following her husband and his brother, who would be driving the moving truck with our combined belongings. Would Logan be able to endure sitting still that long?

My daughter suggested I ask his pediatrician for a mild sedative. I was hesitant, as I viewed medication as a last resort, and only when necessary, but when I consulted the doctor during our last pediatric visit before our move, he prescribed something and told me to just use it as needed.

May 2010, the month before our move, was a whirlwind of activity. It was the last month of the school year, which included parent/teacher conferences, an IEP meeting, school programs and appreciations, and gathering all the paperwork I could to take along with me for reference. We also visited the pediatrician and a dentist for a final checkup and to collect his medical records to pass on to his new providers, although the dental checkup did not work out as planned. He refused to get in the chair, so the dentist suggested waiting and trying to find a dentist in our new location. (See Chapter 15.)

We started packing the day after school ended. I had Logan help me pack his toys, so he would know what boxes they were in, keeping out his favorite ones for the trip, of course. He was quite concerned we would be able to take Lasagna, his orange betta-fish, with us. I was quite worried Lasagna might not survive the long trip, but I am happy to report he did. Under Logan's watchful eye, he got to ride with me in the front seat the whole way in the special leak-proof container we'd gotten for him.

Logan did so well during the trip! We only used the medication once, which helped him stay calm and take a nap during the very long drive.

Things started happening very fast once we got to our destination. We arrived in Fayetteville, North Carolina, on May 31. We looked for and miraculously found an apartment for Logan and me on June 1, and moved into our new home in Spring Lake on June 2. Our new two-bedroom apartment had a big open front- and backyard and was located just five minutes from the elementary school he would be attending.

After unloading our belongings, we all went for lunch at Cuppy's Coffee, a small-town coffee shop just across the main road from our new home. Logan loved that place, as it had a big shelf of toys and games available to its clientele. We ended up spending many hours there in the year that followed to play a game of his choice and for well-earned special treats. His favorite? Milk with a large double-chocolate-chip muffin!

CHAPTER 13

Cutting Myself Some Slack

After my daughter and her family left to go unpack their belongings in their new home on Fort Bragg, Logan and I started setting up our new home. His room was first, so he could settle into a somewhat familiar setting with his belongings. I was amazed at how well he seemed to adjust and loved his new room and home. All the preparation ahead of time and involving him in each step of the move paid off. Still, I could tell he was a little anxious, so to give us both a break, I decided to walk down to a "block party" that he had spotted a little way down the road, which included a big bounce house. —His favorite!

I found out the neighborhood event was organized by a small nearby church. I was approached by one of its members and warmly invited to come and join them for the Sunday service. I politely declined and explained that I was taking care of my autistic grandson, who would not be able to sit still through a church service. The lady I was talking to excitedly exclaimed that it would be no problem, as he could attend the Sunday school class of Mrs. Vicky. "Let me introduce you!"

Vicky, who oversaw the Sunday school class, happened to be a school psychologist and quite familiar with autism. While telling her how we'd just arrived from Louisiana and that we were still moving in, she listened attentively to my story and all that had happened over the past few months. "You must be exhausted!" she concluded, and told me that even just for the sake of getting a break I should come to church each Sunday. She would personally take charge of Logan and make sure he was okay.

It honestly sounded too good to be true. I could hardly remember the time I'd done anything without Logan, and she was right, moving had left me so tired. Self-care had not been on my radar for as long as I could remember, and listening to Vicky talk about how important that was resonated.

I ended up attending the small "Blue Church," as Logan called it, led by Pastor Clyde and his wife Ellen, almost every week. Vicky was always there to take care of Logan, who I know was a handful to keep tabs on and sometimes catch. He was a runner, and on more than one occasion he'd dash out the Sunday school room and down the aisle to the front of the sanctuary to bang out a tune on the piano, which fascinated him. The first time this happened I held my breath, afraid of the reaction he and I might get. I shouldn't have, because the pastor and congregation took the interruption in stride and with good humor.

Those few hours each Sunday morning became a highlight, and as Vicky predicted, provided some of the rest and refueling I needed. It was also an opportunity for Logan to play with other children. He was able to join some of his new friends for Vacation Bible School activities that summer too, providing me with additional respite. This was the beginning of learning to take better care of myself in other ways also.

Reflecting on self-care, I realized that one reason for not taking time to relax and recharge was that I'd always been a perfectionist. When I was a new parent, I would set out my eldest son's ironed clothes for the next day, polish his little leather shoes, and make sure the play area and house were spotless. I took pride in having a clean, nearly "perfect" home, and in having my boy look his very best.

When number two came along, I didn't keep up quite as well, but let's say the clothes were ironed every other day, and the shoes polished not as often.

With number three, I still tried to keep some semblance of order, and the kids still looked neat and clean, but perfection went out the door. I don't think I have to tell you what happened when numbers four, five, and six arrived.

Fast-forward twenty-some years, when I started caring for 6-month-old Logan. At first, I tried my best to revive those days of perfection and have things in tip-top shape. However, Logan was a handful, more so than any of my other children had ever been. I didn't know then that his hyperactivity and frequent crying were due to his autism and sensory issues, which weren't officially diagnosed until later.

Once I learned more about autism and the importance of

early intervention, my tendency for perfection kicked in once again. I was determined to do the very best for him and tried to follow every instruction from his teachers and therapists to a T. Additionally, I read whatever book, blog, or article I could get my hands on, and tried to participate in any social activities the best I could as well.

After a while, it became obvious that I was not going to be able to keep up, physically and emotionally, with all the demands that come with caring for a child with autism. I was stretched to the limit, and something had to give.

Next to having the sole care of my grandson and having to keep up with the little remote editing work I still did, the pressures of managing school meetings and IEPs to find solutions to numerous incidents, doctor's and dentist appointments, and the need to work around other family-related issues were getting to me. I knew I needed respite, but my circumstances hardly afforded it. Funds were tight, and I didn't have anyone to help or give me a break from time to time. Still, I knew I needed it!

When I thought about it more, I realized I needed a mindset change first. In my desire to do everything so perfectly and give Logan the very best at every opportunity, I was overextending myself. I had to come to grips with the fact that even if I had to skip an activity and do something simpler, like putting my feet up and sitting in the backyard with a cup of tea while my grandson chased butterflies and collected bugs, it was not going to hurt him. It did both of us a world of good.

One of the key things that helped me find a better balance in taking care of Logan and taking care of myself was learning to ask for help and accept it when it was offered. I always felt bad about asking others to take care of Logan, and often declined offers that would have afforded me a break. Besides not wanting to burden others, it took me a while to realize that it also had to do with trusting others with him. I raised him and knew him in and out, and I worried that others might not recognize some of the things that led to meltdowns, or if he had one, would know how to bring him out of it. I loved him so much and didn't want him to have to go through anything that might be difficult for him. But in being so protective, I realized I was robbing him of some great learning opportunities—and robbing myself of much-needed rest.

Starting to attend that small community church in our neighborhood was the first in a series of decisions I made to take better care of myself. I was hesitant at first, as I was not sure how Vicky and her staff would be able to handle Logan along with the other children, but I was pleasantly surprised at how well it went. Even if they didn't handle every situation "perfectly" or the way I would, it was a good opportunity for my grandson to play with other children, and for me to get a break and make new friends.

Learning to cut myself some slack has been an ongoing process ever since—and I am still learning.

The Importance of Self-Care

Hectic schedules can drain your energy and keep you so busy that you often forget to take care of yourself both physically and emotionally. Take a moment to stop and think about what you need to do to be able to perform at your very best. Regular self-care can improve your well-being and self-esteem. It also increases the resiliency that you need to help bounce back when problems arise.

So, what does self-care look like, and what can you do?

- **Tell yourself that you matter;** and because you matter, it is important to spend time and energy on helping yourself feel better. Self-care is finding a way to build yourself up.
- **Be extra nice to yourself.** Do things that you enjoy and that help you to relax and unwind.
- **Be patient with yourself.** Accept that you will make mistakes; know that you can't please everyone. Know that things will get better, even though it might take a while.
- **Invest in yourself.** Follow your dreams. Study or read about things that interest you.
- **Recognize when you are in over your head.** Sometimes this means that you need to admit that you need someone to throw you a safety line; this could include working with a therapist, talking to a trusted adult, or going to a support group.
- **Say no to situations or people that you know could**

negatively trigger you. Self-care means that you protect yourself so you can build a stronger future self.

- **Think about things that happened in the past, and learn from them** so you don't repeat the same pattern. Self-care means taking time to evaluate if situations and relationships are healthy and if they should continue.

- **Focus forward.** Self-care means moving ahead, not looking back. Making goals for tomorrow or next week is your first step toward the future.

- **Be proud of yourself.** Declare victory when things go well. Recognize when you make good choices or when you succeed at something that you have been working toward.

The next time you hear "take care of yourself," remember these nine points. They can make a difference in your life and result in a stronger YOU!

Additional Ideas for Easy, Affordable Self-Care

- **Incorporate activities that you like,** even when you don't feel like it. Listen to music, work in the garden, engage in a hobby—whatever it is that you enjoy.

- **Pamper yourself.** Take a warm bath and light candles. Read a nice book, or go out for dinner occasionally with family or a close friend.

- **Eat balanced meals** to take care of your body. For those who like to cook, preparing a favorite dish can be therapeutic.

- **Find time to exercise,** even if it's a short walk every day. I used to take a "nature walk" with Logan almost daily, weather permitting.

- **Sleep at least 7 hours a night** as often as possible. You need rest to be your best.

- **Laughter is the best medicine.** Buy a lighthearted book or watch a comedy. Whenever you can, try to find some humor in everyday situations.

- **Keep a journal.** Write down your thoughts and feelings. This helps provide perspective on your situation and serves as an important release for your emotions.

- **Arrange telephone contact** with a family member, a friend, advocate, or a volunteer so that someone calls regularly to be sure everything is all right. You can ask this person for help with contacting other family members or let them know if you need anything.

- **Try to set a time for afternoons or evenings out,** and ask a family member or friend to be a sitter.

- **Seek out friends and family to help you** so that you can have some time away from the home. If it is difficult to leave, invite friends and family over to visit with you. Share some tea or coffee. You must interact with others.

- Last, but certainly not least, **permit yourself to rest** and to do things that you enjoy daily. You will be a better parent or caregiver for it.

CHAPTER **14**

Doctor's Visits and Vaccinations

Most schools require a medical checkup before the start of school, especially when you come from out of state. Whether it's a school-required checkup or a child's yearly visit, it can be a challenge to make it through one without a meltdown, especially if a blood draw and/or vaccinations are in order.

Even before Logan was diagnosed with autism, doctor's visits were very difficult! I didn't know then that he had sensory processing disorder, and I was puzzled as to why it was so hard for him to have his ears, nose, and throat checked. He was terrified of the doctor's office, and when he was due for a blood draw or vaccinations, because he was so big and strong, it took two or more people to hold him down. It unnerved me every time and I felt so bad for him!

Once he was diagnosed, it explained many of these behaviors, but I was still at a loss as to how to make this better for him and not such a traumatic experience. I researched it and found terrific information and a free tool kit on the Autism Speaks website. I also found some great information and free visual supports for visits to the doctor and dentist online.

I printed out the visual supports and talked with Logan about each part of the doctor's visit ahead of time. I told him he could carry his "checklist" and check off each step of our visit himself. He loved feeling in charge like that.

Since we had just moved and would be visiting a new doctor, I also called the doctor's office ahead of time and emailed them a copy of the checklist I would be using with Logan. They were very understanding and extremely accommodating when we arrived. Wait time was kept short for us, and both the nurse and doctor were patient and took their time with him.

The first time I used this checklist, my grandson was still fearful of lying or sitting on the examination table and allowing the doctor to touch his belly, listen to his heart and lungs, and look at his eyes, throat, and ears. I asked the doctor if she could model what she was going to do to him on me first, and that did the trick. When he saw it was not hurting me, and would not hurt him, he cooperated, and we chalked it up as a success.

Once all done, his favorite part of the visit was going to the Dollar General store around the corner to get his reward—another set of foam "grow capsule bugs," which were his favorite incentive at the time.

Each visit to the doctor since then I prepared him with the same "checklist," and each time it went better, to the point that even the blood draw, while by no means his favorite, transpired without a major meltdown! He knew it would just hurt for a moment—and the reward he would receive afterward outweighed the discomfort. It pays to prepare!

Doctor's Visit Visual Support

MY VISIT TO THE DOCTOR

	Go to the doctor	
	Wait in the waiting room	
	Listen to music	
	Take height and weight	
	Take blood pressure	
	Wait in the exam room	
	Doctor's exam	
	Say goodbye	
	Get treat!	

CHAPTER 15

First Successful Visit to the Dentist

I approached Logan's visit to the dentist with some trepidation. I had attempted to take him to the dentist before we moved, but it had been impossible to even get him into the chair.

When he was little, brushing his teeth was a major daily challenge. Still, with persistence, and experimenting with the brush and toothpaste he liked best, we had settled into a good routine. He would gingerly "brush" a little bit, and I would finish by standing behind him, holding his chin with one hand, and gently brushing until all his teeth were clean and free from "sugar bugs."

He only tolerated very little toothpaste on his brush, which I rubbed into the bristles with my finger, so he'd hardly see it, because if the gel or paste was on top of the bristles, he always protested. It must have been something about the texture or taste that made it hard for him to handle.

I knew his first checkup would include the hygienist brushing his teeth and applying fluoride, so I was concerned it wouldn't turn into a scene. I researched a bit and found Autism Speaks' very helpful Dental Tool Kit, which has excellent advice that can be passed on to the dentist ahead of time.

I called several local dentists before I settled on one who understood and was willing to accommodate my special requests for Logan's first visit. I emailed and sent information about autism and his needs ahead of time, which they read and acknowledged.

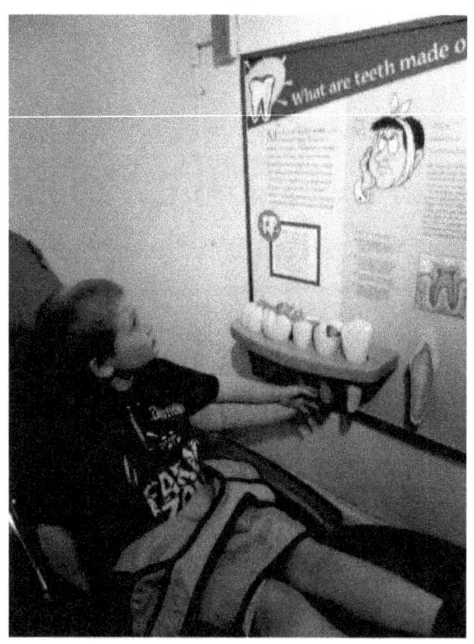

Just after we arranged the appointment, we happened to visit the local children's museum, which included a "dentist's office" with a real chair that went up and down, an X-ray apron, and some of the "tools" a dentist uses. It was perfect visual preparation for his upcoming appointment. I also prepared at home by writing a picture story for Logan, which we went over repeatedly, and which he carried with him to refer to during his checkup.

The staff was so accommodating, and they took their time to reassure him and make sure he was comfortable with everything they were going to do during the checkup. I'd asked if I could bring the toothpaste he used at home, which they said was fine, and they were careful to show him that they'd just used a little bit.

It took a little longer than a regular trip to the dentist might take, but all the preparation paid off, and his first visit was a pleasant experience for him, paving the way for future successful visits.

10 Tips to Prepare for a Trip to the Dentist

Going to the dentist can be scary for any child, but especially for a child with autism. Taking some extra time to prepare your child for the visit and transitions during his time at the dentist's office will help to eliminate a lot of anxiety and stress for both you and your child. Here's how:

- Find a good, and preferably a recommended pediatric dentist in your area.
- Meet with the dentist ahead of time to explain your child's unique needs.
- Ask the dentist what will take place during your child's visit and make a step-by-step list.
- If possible, take pictures of the dentist's office, the equipment that will be used, and the people your child will meet.
- Create a short social story/picture schedule for your child of each step that the trip to the dentist will include. (If you were not able to take photos, you can download a free picture schedule at www.do2learn.com.)
- If possible, take your child to the dentist's office once before the actual appointment to meet the dentist and staff and to familiarize him/her with the sights, sounds, and smells of the place, which can be challenging for a child with sensory issues.

- Bring your child's favorite toy, music to listen to, or fidgets to keep him busy during the exam.
- If loud sounds are an issue, bring some earplugs or noise-dampening earphones.
- If bright lights bother your child, bring and allow your child to wear sunglasses inside.

For more detailed information about going to the dentist, check out the dental tool kit by Autism Speaks on www.autismspeaks.org.

CHAPTER 16

Daily Challenges

As every parent experiences, whether a child is on the autism spectrum or not, taking care of young children is a big and full-time job. The daily challenges can sometimes be overwhelming, and with an autistic child, these can be magnified even more.

Taking Logan for a haircut was one of those challenges. He never liked getting his hair cut, and from very young the feel and the sound of the buzzer, or seeing the scissors coming near him would trigger a full-blown meltdown. When very young, I would sit him on my lap and hold his arms so the hairdresser could quickly trim his locks, but even then, he would scream the whole time. However, with him getting older and bigger, this wasn't working anymore, so I needed to find a different solution.

One day, I stopped by the hair salon in the small strip mall near our house. I explained my situation to the owner and asked if she would be up to trying to give Logan's hair a trim. I could not have asked for a better response. She got down on Logan's level, smiled sweetly at him, and in a soft tone asked him if he'd like to check out her special, colored clippers and aprons. She handed him the clippers to feel, first off and then on, showed him the different aprons, and then told him he could pick which one to use for his haircut. He picked a blue clipper and an apron with penguins on it. I watched with tears in my eyes as she lifted him onto the booster seat and started to trim his hair. Whenever he would cringe a little, she'd stop and acknowledge his discomfort and ask permission to continue. "Okay," he'd say. He'd never sat through a haircut without crying before, but he did this time.

Needless to say, this is where Logan got his haircuts from then on, and so did I. Once Logan was done, it was my turn. She locked the front door of the shop so he would not be able to elope, and had one of her staff sit with Logan as he watched his favorite TV show, so I could get my haircut. She was the best hairdresser ever, and her patience with Logan amazed me. I later learned her daughter had a child with a disability, which explained her exceptional capability to understand Logan and his needs.

CHAPTER 17

School Transitions

During the summer vacation, Logan and I had lots of fun together. We spent time with his cousins and enjoyed visits from one of his uncles and another great-aunt. We also continued to frequent Cuppy's Coffee, one of our favorite hangouts.

One day while there, I couldn't help but overhear the conversation of a group of women sitting at an adjoining table. There were numerous references to autism, and one of the ladies kept looking over at Logan playing with his toys next to me while I was drinking my cherished morning coffee. When the ladies finished their meeting, she came over to me and introduced herself.

Amy asked if Logan had autism, and when I confirmed he did, she told me she was the mother of Haven, her autistic daughter, and that she worked as an autism resource specialist with the Autism Society of North Carolina

(ASNC). The meeting she'd attended was with the women of their Harnett County chapter. We were soon engrossed in conversation, and we parted with the promise to keep in touch.

Meeting Amy couldn't have been timelier, as I needed all the help I could get with preparing Logan for kindergarten in his new school.

Soon after, Amy invited me to attend a back-to-school workshop at their ASNC office. Childcare would be provided, she promised, so I would be able to focus my attention on the meeting. I am so happy I went, because what I learned that day not only helped Logan transition back to school that year but many other families, as over the years I shared this helpful information with numerous other parents, caregivers, and teachers.

Amy and I both felt our initial meeting that day was simply meant to be, and we remain friends to this day.

Back-To-School Checklist

- Contact the school and staff before the start of the school year
- Write a story for your child including school rules and expectations
- Prepare your child at home by reviewing the story often
- Request orientation accommodations if needed
- Meet with the teacher and aides and introduce them to your child
- Request schedule, event, and activity information ahead of time
- Prepare a visual schedule for your child and review it before the start of school and before each school day.

CHAPTER 18

Getting Ready for the First Day of School

Before the start of the kindergarten school year, I contacted the school and requested a time to visit. I explained that because my grandson has autism, I would like to meet regarding his placement, and arrange to see his new classroom and meet with his new teacher, if possible.

I've done this with every school he went to since, and like this school, most of the schools I contacted over the years reacted positively to my request. It helped the transition back to school, or to a new school, go much more smoothly.

It also helped lay the groundwork for good communication with the school staff. From the start, the staff knew I was going to be an involved grandparent, with a desire for open, two-way discussion about my grandson's needs and progress.

Once all the paperwork was processed and his placement

worked out, I was able to walk through the new school with Logan before school started, to give him an idea of the layout and where his classroom and desk would be. I also asked permission to take pictures, so I would be able to write a picture story for him about his new school and classroom. The staff happily obliged.

It helped Logan to feel a lot less anxious about the big change of going back to school in a new town, as his arrival in a new school on the first day back was not going to be a complete unknown.

During the month leading up to the first day of school, we spent time talking about school daily. We reviewed his "My New School" story and often talked about school rules.

Most children with autism are visual learners, and my grandson is no exception, so using clip art and my printer, I created several key-ring cards to prepare my grandson for what would be expected of him at school. "Repetition is the law of memory" for any of us; and especially for children with autism, the more they see and hear something, the better they will remember. By the time school started, Logan had the school rules memorized.

This may vary in different locations, but the school Logan was going to attend had an orientation day for parents and students before the start of school. Some schools have the parents and students come in to meet with their new teacher and an aide(s) personally, staggering the visits at ten-minute intervals, while other schools may invite groups of parents and students to meet at the same time.

In this particular school, the orientation day promised to be quite a chaotic event, and the confusion and presence of so many people in one room seemed to be the perfect setting for a potential meltdown. I called ahead of time and asked if there would be a way for my grandson and me to meet privately ahead of the group orientation. After some persistence on my part, the request was kindly granted.

If for some reason your child was not able to meet his new teacher before the start of school, a good alternative could be to request a phone or video conference. Some schools may allow you to invite your child's teacher to visit you at home, or you may be able to arrange another time for you and your child to meet the teacher at school or another location.

Meeting with the teacher provides an opportunity to pass on any information about your child that you feel will be helpful, including copies of any visual supports your child may be using at home.

Because we'd opted out of the orientation event, and Logan's new teacher was not available at the time we went for a walk-through of Logan's new school, I had left her a note and asked her to call me, because I would love for Logan to meet her before the start of school. When she called, I invited her for a cup of coffee at our home, which she happily agreed to after checking with the principal about it. We had a great visit together, and she and my grandson had an instant connection.

I showed her the visual supports my grandson had used in his previous school setting, which I had copied for her, and I was able to answer other questions she had as well. She had a chance to observe my grandson during her visit, which gave her an idea of his communication abilities at the time.

Just in case I had not been able to meet with her, I had also prepared an "All About..." page and a "Positive Student Profile," both of which included at least one recent photo of Logan. I received copies of these forms when I attended the workshop organized by Amy and the Autism Society of North Carolina. Amy had shared how this helped new teachers and aides to get to know her autistic daughter and provided them with important information about her to keep on file to refer to if needed.

While Logan has been in my care, I have filled out these two forms for his teachers each time he started a new school year, including his recent freshman high school year. It never failed to impress and generate gratitude. Things the teacher and aide otherwise would have to find out by trial and error were already covered and helped start their interaction with their new student on a positive note.

Starting school also means a big change in a child's daily routine and schedule. To prepare Logan for what his day was going to be like, including transitions from one activity to another, I asked his teacher if she could give me his daily and weekly schedule ahead of time, and she provided me with all the information needed. She also tried to stay on top of letting me know about any schedule changes ahead of time.

I then printed lined slips of paper, called "Logan's Day," and each morning we included in our routine of getting dressed, eating breakfast, and brushing teeth, the writing out of his daily schedule.

Logan took his written daily schedule to school with him, and the teacher always placed it in the same spot, so he could cross off the different activities before transitioning to the next one. It worked like a charm most of the time!

Sample Back-to-School Story

Following is a sample of the story I wrote and printed out for Logan before he started kindergarten. It included the pictures I took while we visited his new school and classroom and pictures of his new teacher and her aide. I reviewed this story often with him during the days leading up to the first day of school. He was so excited once the big day arrived.

My new school

This is my new school (picture). The name of my new school is … My new school's mascot is a … (picture).

My new classroom

This is my new kindergarten classroom (picture). I will have new friends in my classroom. I will be a good friend. Good friends are nice to each other. I will have lots of fun with my new friends. I like my new classroom!

This is one of the bathrooms (picture). I will go to the bathroom all by myself. When I flush the toilet, it may be a little bit loud, but that's OK. I can cover my ears, and I will be brave, like ... (in my grandson's case, his betta fish Lasagna).

My new teachers

My new kindergarten teacher is Ms. … (picture). Her assistant is Ms. … (picture). An assistant is a helper. I will learn many new things from my teachers. I will be a good student and listen carefully when Ms. … and Ms. … tell me things.

At school, I will be a 5-Star Listener. My eyes are watching, my ears are listening, my lips are closed, my hands are still, and my feet are quiet when it is time to listen. Listening to my teacher and following the rules is good. I will be a good student.

CHAPTER 19

Autism Is...?

It was during this summer that Logan started asking me questions about autism. During my meetings with different people, he often heard me use the "autism" word when talking about him, and on one such occasion he pulled my sleeve and asked me, "Grandma, autism is...?" His inquisitive mind wanted to know, so I wanted to explain it to him clearly and positively. I promised him I would explain it to him a little later when we'd have some time to talk about it.

That night, while lying in bed, wondering how to best tell him what it meant to have autism, the idea came to me to present it to him in poem format, as he was into rhyming words at the time. The beginning of a verse formed in my mind, so I got up and started writing. Before long, the first draft of the *Autism Is...?* book was born. When I read it to him the next day, he loved it. He wanted to read it over and over. I typed it up and printed it for him, but that printout was soon worn out, warranting a new one.

When I later showed it to Amy, she encouraged me to publish it to help other parents and caregivers explain the autism diagnosis to their children. That didn't happen for a while, but eventually I did, along with other rhyming stories I wrote for Logan to help explain other topics he had questions about. Little did I know that of all my books, *Autism Is...?* would become a favorite and best-seller.

Explaining the autism diagnosis to children on the spectrum can be controversial. Some parents worry that an autism label may cause their child to feel they are broken or less than others, or in other cases, they may worry their child may use the autism diagnosis as an excuse to give up and not try. Issues such as this can come up, of course, but they can be addressed if needed.

Individuals with autism who were not told until they were adults often share that not understanding and knowing led to poor interactions with others, isolation, ridicule, and sometimes to feeling they were a disappointment and failure to their families and others.

Logan's reaction to having autism has not been anything like that, and if anything, he has been proud of his autism. Giving him information about his diagnosis has helped him accept himself and appreciate his uniqueness. He knows he is different, but not less! I hope that as he grows and matures, this information will help him succeed and spur him on to be the best he can be in life.

There is no "correct" age or a blueprint on how to tell a child about their autism. However, if a child is asking questions, it's best to answer them as soon as possible. I needed a little time to prepare my answer when Logan asked, but I knew that postponing talking about it would only increase his anxiety.

You may or may not wish to explain autism to your child at such a young age, but if you do, I hope the book I wrote for him can help make it easier for you to broach the subject, as it did for me when explaining autism to Logan. Once he read the story, even before it was illustrated, he was satisfied with the answer, and even today, as a teenager, he refers to "his book" and his autism positively and with pride.

CHAPTER 20

Safety First

When browsing the news one day, my heart almost stopped when I saw the headline, "The Dangers of Wandering Kids: Autism Community Mourns Three Drowning Deaths in One Week." After describing these heartbreaking incidents, the article called for more attention and research into what causes children with autism to wander or elope. This can be a huge issue for many families, as it was for me.

Ever since he started walking, Logan was a runner—and a fast one at that! He would impulsively take off, and because he lacked a sense of danger, he often darted toward the street or some other place where it is not safe to run. Keeping him safe while out in the community became one of my biggest concerns, because I could hardly keep or catch up with him.

One heart-stopping incident was when he ran out of the front yard directly toward the street and in front of an oncoming car. Thankfully, the driver kept to the speed limit of our residential neighborhood, and he was able to stop just inches from him. The driver was shaken up and mad, and I was shaken too, as I just hadn't seen that one coming. One moment we were sitting together on the front porch, enjoying a lovely spring day, and the next he was standing in front of that car, showing absolutely no fear or awareness of danger.

Logan also loved the water! He would jump into a pool without a second thought. Whenever we went swimming, I would put water wings on him, of course, but he inevitably would try to make a run for any body of water we'd pass on walks or during outings.

Another incident happened about a year later when Logan was 5 years old. We used to get our haircuts at the same hairdresser, who was always very accommodating of his sensory needs. (See Chapter 16.) She would lock her shop door that led to the busy parking area out front and would ask one of her employees to make sure he was playing or watching TV while it was my turn in the chair.

One day, however, one of the employees forgot to lock the door behind an incoming customer, and he made a run for it. Before we knew it, he was out the door and running into the grocery store next door. Thankfully, he didn't run onto the road or into the parking lot, and we were able to catch up with him quickly. Still, the incident could have ended differently.

At one point, the running incidents were so frequent that I researched safety leashes, and I bought one that looked like a good temporary solution. One end attached to his belt loop, while the other end had a band that closed around my wrist with Velcro. It provided plenty of freedom of movement for him as the leash was quite long, but at the same time, he could not run away from me. Logan seemed to like it too, as he could walk independently while we were out in public places, without him having to hold my hand.

Did I get some stares? Sure! Did some people question me about it? Oh, yes! Did I let it bother me? It did a little at first, but I soon realized that whenever confronted or asked about the leash I had the opportunity to explain it and create greater awareness about autism. People's reactions were usually positive and supportive. One grandmother commented, "My grandkids don't have autism, but I might get one for my 3-year-old granddaughter! She always runs off and is so fast that I can barely catch up with her."

Logan also needed to learn to stay safe while in the car. One day, while in his car seat in my daughter's minivan, he unbuckled himself while we were driving and tried to open the side sliding door. Thankfully, we were able to stop him and pull over, but it was a sobering reminder to us to always have the child-lock enabled on the back doors of any vehicle and to teach Logan safety rules while riding in a car. I created a simple visual that listed the "car rules" and reviewed them constantly every time we got into the car.

It was not easy to teach Logan some of these basic safety rules, which is why I wrote another story for him. I later published it in his *Danger Is…?* book. We read and reviewed the "10 Danger Rules" in the book so often that he eventually memorized them, and after some time his impulsive running decreased. He still behaved unsafely from time to time, but when reminded of the rules, he was redirected much easier.

Like Logan, many children with autism lack fear and a sense of danger, and it can be difficult to teach them about safety. Visually and verbally reviewing safety rules regularly, and especially before going out, is very important and will reinforce the importance of safe behavior.

When Logan got older, he also learned to swim, which is another key to keeping autistic children safe. Many are drawn to water, and therefore nearby bodies of water are often the first place first responders will look when an autistic child is reported missing. Many programs provide swim lessons for children with special needs at no or little cost. Logan was able to join such a free program when he was 6 years old and is now a good swimmer. Knowing he can stay afloat and get out of the water when needed is reassuring.

Another important safety measure is to keep cleaning agents, medications, and other poisonous or toxic materials out of reach of autistic children—and not just when they are very young. Even when older, their curiosity may get the best of them, and without a sense of danger, they could easily ingest a chemical substance—including ones with pictures of crossbones on them. This symbol often invokes the image of pirates as it is used in comic books and movies on pirate ships and flags, and many children may not associate this picture with poison anymore.

For this reason, Penn State University initiated a Pesticide Education Program introducing the image of Mr. Yuk. In my opinion, this is a far more effective visual to demonstrate to children that something is poisonous, and I have  used their stickers of Mr. Yuk for quite some time now.

Keeping Logan safe has been no small feat, and it took a lot of work and repetition, but it has paid off in him being more aware of his surroundings and behaving more responsibly and safely at home, at school, and while out in the community.

Safety Tips

Be Proactive

"Prevention is worth a pound of cure." Be prepared! Have a plan! How well can you explain how ASD affects your child should you need to explain it to the authorities in case your child elopes? What if you are panicking? Don't be isolated; decide what to tell neighbors and share your concerns with them. Contact local first responders to set up a time to meet with them. Introduce them to your child, and/or provide them with a photo of your child.

Think Ahead

Have a written plan, including emergency contact numbers, how your child communicates, what your child is attracted to, what his/her triggers are, their favorite toys, songs, foods, medications, allergies, or other medical information, and what might calm your child if he/she should get upset or hurt.

This informational handout can be always copied and carried with you—at home, in your car, and in your purse or wallet. Circulate this handout to family members, trusted neighbors, friends, and co-workers, in case you become incapacitated or injured while caring for a person with autism at home or in the community. This information will also come in handy if you are in an area other than your neighborhood and are approached by the police.

If wandering is a concern, provide a copy of this information to law enforcement, fire agencies, and EMS.

Ask your local 911 call center to "red flag" this information in their database. In case of an emergency, dispatchers can alert patrol officers about your concerns before the officers arrive. When we provide police officers with key information before an incident occurs, we can expect better responses.

Plan Ahead

For out-of-the-ordinary events—family reunions, field trips, birthday parties, and community outings—who will keep your child safe? Scope out environments ahead of time for potential safety issues. Avoid or be prepared to cut short activities that might be difficult, or get respite for your child. Call ahead to venues for accommodations (long lines), or "check in" ahead of time to allow time for transitioning into a new situation.

Prepare Your Child

What can your child learn? Can he/she recognize stop and exit signs, or other verbal and visual cues? Consider ID bracelets or temporary tattoos. Can your child read and is he/she able to learn to follow written rules? Create visuals and social narratives.

Get copies of safety behaviors and rules in schools, and get copies of fire drills and other school safety procedures so you can review them with your child. Perhaps create visuals of the rules. Also, be sure to include safety goals in Individual Education Plans (IEPs).

Practicing fire escapes or emergency drills in your home through role-play, visuals, and frequent reviews are also key to keeping children safe.

Resources

There are many free or inexpensive safety kits on the market that can be used to record and share information about your child with family members, neighbors, and first responders. Here's the link to the free online *Safe in the Community* kit that I used: https://www.autismsociety-nc.org/introducing-our-online-safe-in-the-community-kit/

CHAPTER 21

Starting Kindergarten

Despite all the preparation, Logan had a rough start in his kindergarten class. Like in his previous preschool setting, he was in a regular classroom and had scheduled times for special education, speech, and occupational therapy. I soon found out, however, that this school and its teachers were not nearly as prepared and trained for special needs students as the staff of his preschool at Fort Polk.

His teacher, though well-meaning and experienced as a regular education teacher, had little or no understanding of autism, and it soon started showing in Logan's behavior. He started bolting out of the classroom, running the long hallways, and disrupting the lessons. Her aide was doing her best to help Logan, but she also was not trained and often unavailable. The teacher approached me one day and asked me if I had considered putting Logan on medication. I was taken aback by her question and later asked Amy about it.

When I explained to her what was happening in the classroom, she told me that it is not a teacher's place to suggest medication and that the best way to respond to both her question and Logan's challenging behavior was with a letter, so there would be a paper trail and proper record of my concerns.

This is the letter I wrote to Logan's teacher and her assistant:

Dear Mrs. T. and Mrs. M.,

Thank you so much for all you are doing for Logan and all the children. I admire you for the HUGE job you do with so many children in your classroom. I realize it's quite an adjustment for you and him, and you are in my thoughts daily. Please don't hesitate to tell me if there is anything I can do to make things easier.

You asked me if I had considered medication for Logan, so I wanted to tell you that I have. In researching the possibility, I found and was told that the best way to go about this would be to travel back and forth to Raleigh to get an evaluation and medication option worked out for Logan. Putting an autistic child on medication is complicated, as what works for one does not for another, and it would mean testing things out and seeing how it works over time. I feel at this point that it would be better to wait on this, as besides Logan trying to adjust to school, he would also have to undergo testing and doctor's trips, which makes for a lot of stress for all involved.

Maybe one thing that would help right now is to keep showing Logan his schedule by using his schedule stick, as he is a visual learner. He does not respond very well to spoken instructions, mainly because his brain keeps firing away, and he does not register what he is hearing. Holding up the schedule, repeating the word on it, and keeping that in front of him on his desk, whether the stick or the written schedule or both, might help settle him quicker. Because he is so excited about his new school and classroom, I don't think he will use the list or schedule on his own, but he does well if it is shown to him.

Writing a word of instruction on his drawing board might help also if it's something different you want him to do. For example, if he needs to be quiet or sit down, just the word Quiet or Sit might help. I use that at home to move him along at times, and it does settle him. He also has a magnetic schedule on the fridge that I use for transitioning when needed.

I am enclosing something I compiled for a friend with some basic autism information. You may already be aware of most of it, but I thought to give you a copy just in case it can be helpful.

Thank you for all you do, and again, please let me know if there is anything else I can do to help.

Mrs. T. did try, but Logan still struggled. This soon required a meeting with Ron, the county's school psychologist and head of the Autism Problem Solving Committee.

I was again thankful to have Amy as a soundboard and support during our meetings. She understood where I was coming from when I voiced my disappointment when it was suggested that Logan join a self-contained special education classroom.

In a conversation I had with her recently, she recalled this incident and told me Ron had been a little annoyed at my resistance and asked her why I was so against and upset about Logan moving to a self-contained classroom. He just didn't understand my reservations, as it was not going well in the inclusive setting.

She explained to him that to me this move simply felt like I'd failed. I had worked so hard and long to prepare Logan, and he'd made so much progress in his previous school, that this seemed like a step back instead of forward and made me feel that my best had not been good enough. She hit the nail on the head, as this is exactly what I was going through.

When I finally agreed to give the self-contained setting a try, little did I know that this was the beginning of a series of challenges and a long and hard fight to provide Logan, as well as the other children in his classroom, with the appropriate services that they all needed and deserved.

In the months that followed, I had many conversations and meetings with Ron about this, and he became my greatest ally. His insight and advice meant so much, and the school rules he and his team later developed and presented to Logan's classroom were the inspiration and became the basis for my *School Rules Are…?* book.

CHAPTER 22

IEP Meetings

Since Logan came from Louisiana with an Individual Education Plan (IEP), the first meeting to confirm his current setting was to occur 30 days after starting the school year. I had only attended one IEP before, and I had felt quite comfortable with it as I had already gotten to know everyone at his previous school. However, I was very nervous about this first meeting and was so glad I was able to talk to Amy about the meeting beforehand.

She suggested I get a copy of *All About IEPs—Answers to Frequently Asked Questions About IEPs*, by Peter and Pamela Wright, and Sandra Webb O'Connor (Wrightslaw). This book is perfect and has been my go-to and blueprint for every IEP meeting since. It answered so many of the questions I had and helped me understand what to expect and what should be included in Logan's IEP.

I prepared a list of things I wanted to discuss ahead of

time, which Amy reviewed and helped me tweak, and she suggested I send it to Logan's educational team ahead of time. She also offered to accompany me to the meeting as an advocate. I was so relieved I would not have to go alone, and could not have asked for a better person to accompany me.

Since it looked like it might end up being quite a long meeting, as there was so much to discuss initially, I decided to bake one of my signature Dutch apple pies to express my appreciation for all the members of Logan's team. Teachers, and especially special education teachers and therapists, work very hard and have the best interests of their students at heart. Even though there may be different points of view expressed in an IEP meeting, it's important to remember all members are working toward the same goal—success for the student they are discussing. I wanted to make sure that even though I came with a long list of questions and requests, that the members of Logan's team felt respected and appreciated.

The first meeting was long, and at the end, I was presented with the documents to sign. So much had been discussed that I felt a little uncomfortable with signing right there and then. Amy had told me beforehand that I could request to take the documents home for review, to make sure everything had been recorded and concluded accurately and the way we had all agreed on, so that's what I did.

My request came as a surprise to most of the team, as most parents do not ask for this. If it were not for Amy's encouragement, I wouldn't have either, because in truth, attending an IEP meeting with so many professionals can be very intimidating. Parents may very well feel that the educational team knows best, so who are they to question.

However, parents and caregivers are often their child's best therapists, because they know their child best. They may catch things in the meeting notes that have been recorded inaccurately, or a goal that has not been described clearly.

This was the case with Logan's IEP, which I reviewed with Amy. I told her I did not feel comfortable with some of the wording in Logan's Behavior Intervention Plan (BIP) and with some of the descriptions of his other goals. She agreed that the wording did not accurately reflect the discussion we had, and suggested I put these things in writing. I ended up rewriting some of the goals and interventions and sent my suggestions to the team via email.

As a side note, it is very important that besides expressing concerns verbally, everything is also presented in writing. There must be a clear paper trail for changes to be made and for goals to be effective.

Because there were changes to be made to the IEP, another meeting needed to be called so all could agree to the adjustments. Not everyone had to attend again, and the follow-up meeting was a lot shorter. I of course expressed my heartfelt thanks to everyone for their time and consideration. It was most likely the first time they ever had someone question and request a follow-up meeting to an IEP meeting, and it wasn't the last time. Logan's educational and behavioral progress was very important to me, and before the year was over, we had several other meetings.

10 Tips for Navigating IEP Meetings

One of the most important discussions parents can have with their clinical team is about the goals they have for their children as they grow into adulthood. Most parents grapple with finding the time to think about their child's long-term future when they are facing the daily needs of mealtimes, sleep schedules, or having a successful playdate. However, as tough as this discussion is, it is critically important to start this conversation early because the foundational skills that will enable your child to function well as an adult are taught and acquired during childhood.

A significant part of a child's development will be determined by their school environment, academic placement, and the academic curriculum that guides their learning. A child's initial Individual Education Plan is critical. This important document will lay the groundwork for the types and level of services that a child will receive throughout their academic years. Parents must put sufficient time and effort into preparing for their first and subsequent IEP meetings.

An Individual Education Plan is a legal document that is developed for every child eligible for special education. This plan contains a statement of a child's present level of functioning in terms of performance, educational needs, goals, levels of service, and measurable outcomes. The first IEP meeting is typically held before a child's transition into preschool or as soon as a child is identified as having a special need and determined eligible for special education services.

An IEP meeting can be held at multiple times during the year: after a formal assessment; if a child demonstrates a lack of progress; or if a parent or teacher requests a meeting to develop, review, or revise a child's current IEP.

There are some important steps that parents should consider when beginning the IEP process. We have outlined some of the most important ones for you here. The following guidelines can help you prepare for your first IEP:

- **Understand the IEP process and know your rights.** It is of paramount importance to read up on the IEP process, become familiar with IDEA (Individuals with Disabilities Education Act), and understand your rights as a parent. In addition to studying the law, many parents seek advice from an advocate and network with well-informed parents who have firsthand experience with the IEP process in their school district.

- **Make all your requests in writing.** All requests should be made in writing to create a documentation trail that provides a history of the child's academic needs and requests to the school district (e.g., requests for an IEP meeting, an assessment of any kind, or a classroom placement recommendation). It also allows you to state your requests in your own words. In addition, ask the IEP committee to record these written requests as part of the minutes in an IEP meeting. The IEP committee can accept or deny these requests. If the committee denies the requests, then they must follow the procedural safeguards in

IDEA and provide written notice of why they are denying your request. If the request is not documented in writing, the school district is not required to provide the service. (Be familiar with Prior Notice of the Procedural Safeguards [34 CFR 300.503].)

- **Obtain independent assessments ahead of your IEP meeting.** The school team should not be recommending nor denying services without an assessment to evaluate the need for that service, and neither should parents. You will want to request, in writing, that your child be assessed before the IEP meeting is held. Ideally, if all the necessary assessments are conducted before the IEP meeting, then the recommendations for treatments can be discussed during the IEP meeting. Be sure to request copies of the assessments, progress reports, and proposed goals in advance of the meeting to have ample time to review and be fully informed during the meeting.

- **Organize all your records.** Parents should have all their records on hand and easily accessible during IEP meetings. Create a system of storing and updating all information that makes sense to you and that makes it easy for you to find the information you need.

- **Observe the classroom.** Ask to observe any classroom where your child is being recommended for placement, so you can better understand if it would be a good fit. If for some reason the school will not let you observe, have a professional who is familiar with your child observe the setting. The law states that the team must start with the least restrictive environment (LRE), which is the general education classroom as the first option, and work toward a more restrictive environment only as necessary as needs come up that cannot be met with supports and modifications in the LRE. Therefore, placement should never be decided upon before the child's goals and objectives are concluded.

- **Formulate a list of questions before your IEP.** In advance of the meeting, prepare a comprehensive list of questions (a very long list is completely appropriate). During the meeting, assign someone on your team to take notes and write down answers to all your questions. This allows you to focus on the conversation. A tremendous amount of information is exchanged at IEP meetings, and it can be overwhelming to absorb it all.

- **Make sure goals and objectives are progress oriented.** Goals and objectives are some of the most important elements of an IEP. If the goals and objectives are not written in a manner that is observable and measurable, one cannot determine if a child is making progress. Without this, the school can claim that a child has made progress without producing actual data to evidence the skills gained. In addition, the goals and objectives will specify what a child needs to learn in that academic year. This is the critical time to think more long-term. Will these goals serve where you want your child to be two years from now? Five years from now? Are they laying the foundation for the necessary skills that your child will need as an adult to live the most independent life he or she can? Get input from members of the team that works with your child before the meeting; ask for their opinion of your child's progress and needs.

- **Be the host, not the guest.** Since IEP meetings are held at the school district, parents typically feel like a guest at their child's IEP. However, since the IEP meeting is about your child, parents can create a more personal atmosphere. For example: by providing snacks, pastries, and light refreshments, you can put yourself in the position of host of the IEP meeting. Another idea is to bring a photograph of your child and place it in the center of the table to remind the team who and what the meeting is about—providing services to support this specific child in attaining his or her highest potential.

- **Never go alone.** The support of a family member, uncle, husband, friend, or advocate cannot be overstated. The IEP process can be stressful, tiring, and sometimes overwhelming. Parents often share that having someone else in the room to support them, take notes, and offer reassurance makes a huge difference. In some instances, parents obtain professional support from advocates or special education attorneys who specialize in the IEP process.

- **Disagree without being disagreeable.** Once the team has made their recommendations and concluded the IEP, parents will be asked to sign the IEP document. The IEP document allows for them to sign that they were present at the IEP but that they do not agree at that time with the recommendations. This is a good option to exercise at the end of the meeting. It allows you to take the IEP home to review later and have the option to request changes. This can be done in a very respectful way, allowing you time to make the decisions that are best for your family. As a parent, you are a vital part of your child's IEP team. You are your child's best advocate and the person who knows what's best and most appropriate for him. With the correct information and support, you can create a comprehensive and suitable roadmap for your child's future.

Written by Michelle Stone, MS, BCBA
Author of *A Parent's Guide to the IEP*
Based on an interview with David Wyles

CHAPTER 23

Behavior Is Communication

If there is anything I learned over the years, it is that there are always reasons for behavior and that the autistic child, with the inability to communicate his feelings and needs in conventional ways, is using behavior to tell us something.

For example, besides the teacher in his kindergarten class not being trained or prepared to handle a very active autistic child, he also bolted out of the classroom due to the overstimulating environment. The classroom was overly decorated, with not a bare piece of wall showing anywhere. While neurotypical children may tolerate and even enjoy "busy" décor, this can have an incredibly unsettling effect on children with autism.

This was one of the discussions I had with Ron, and he agreed that this, along with the fact that the large class size generated quite a lot of noise, could have affected Logan's bolting behavior. The self-contained classroom had a much more subdued décor, and there were also fewer students in his room, so I was hopeful that he would be successful.

It didn't take long, however, before I noticed a big change in Logan. He started to come home from school in a very hyper and loud mood, and after only a week, he began to jump on the furniture, including the coffee table. He had never behaved like this, and I wondered what on earth was going on.

One of the following days, while dropping him at school, instead of leaving, I lingered in the hallway for a while to peek into the room through the small window in the door. I was horrified to see that the teacher, a very nice young woman, had no control over the students. She was sitting at her desk while the six or so special needs students, including Logan, were running around the room.

The students ranged in age from kindergarten to 5th grade, and some of the older ones in the classroom were jumping onto chairs and tables, much like I had witnessed Logan doing at home. I realized that he had been mimicking the behavior he had seen at school, which is very common in children on the spectrum.

Naturally, I felt concerned, but I decided to give the situation the benefit of the doubt as perhaps it was just happening at the start of the day, and perhaps later on the children would be learning in an orderly manner. I decided to come and watch later that day, before picking up Logan, and take another look. When I did, it was disheartening to see that the situation was as loud and disorderly as it had been in the morning.

I decided to call Ron and tell him about the situation,

and expressed my concern that Logan, as well as some of the other younger ones, were in the company of much older children who were not necessarily there because of a disability, but because they had been removed from their classes due to behavior problems. It just didn't seem right to me that there was such a large age range and that the younger ones were exposed to behavior that they would be sure to copy.

Ron agreed and was glad I called and promised me he would pay an unexpected visit to evaluate the situation.

CHAPTER 24

Promised Changes and an Appeal

As promised, Ron paid a surprise visit to Logan's classroom after I alerted him to the chaotic circumstances I had witnessed. He agreed that changes were needed, and he assured me that their behavior support person, Ms. Kellie, would be assigned to the classroom to help with some of the behavior issues I had reported.

I was hopeful that after our IEP meeting and my subsequent meetings with Ron, things would improve, but as the months passed, the situation, and subsequently Logan's behavior, regressed instead. I talked to Amy about this often, and after addressing the problems multiple times with Ron, the principal, and other staff at the school, she encouraged me to write a letter to the superintendent.

At this point, I was not just concerned about Logan's education, but also about the other students in his class. None were getting their individual needs met, which broke my heart. The teacher, Ms. M, was well-meaning and wanted to do better, but the constant changing of students in her class and the lack of support from management were very frustrating for her. Special education was just not a priority, and sadly, in this particular school, the tendency was to keep the children with special needs out of sight, and hopefully out of mind. This, however, was not an option for me, and it never will be!

My letter to the superintendent was detailed, polite, and direct. I received an acknowledgment and was told that the director of programs for exceptional children was asked to evaluate this case and that the assistant superintendent of curriculum would also be involved. I anxiously waited for this to happen, but when after three weeks there still was no sign of any action being taken, I sent a follow-up email to express my disappointment.

After this, things finally started happening. The class was restructured and Mrs. Jamie Kostan, the special education lead teacher, relinquished her position as lead to restructure and head up the classroom as Ms. M. was in the process of relocating and accepting a position in another school. Kellie, the behavior specialist, also got involved.

I could not have asked for a better team! Jamie set up the classroom with a visual schedule and other visual supports, provided Logan and all the other students with work on their current level, and established a daily routine that was easy for all the students to follow.

When sometime later I peeked through that little window in the door of the classroom again, I could not believe my eyes. All the students were sitting quietly at their desks, working on their daily assignments. Jamie had a little bell she would ring when it was time for them to switch to another workstation, and they transitioned flawlessly.

Logan's sensory needs were also addressed. He needed movement breaks, but instead of letting him walk all through the classroom and disrupt the other students, she'd marked a big rectangle around his desk with colored tape. Whenever he needed a movement break, she taught him to raise his hand and he would be allowed to walk around his desk for a five-minute interval.

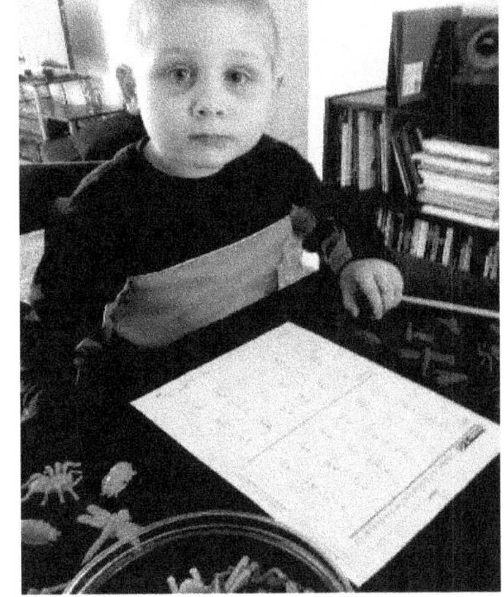

She also discovered that a lot of the behavior Logan had been displaying in class was due to boredom with the work he was given to do. Academically, Logan was way beyond coloring pictures, and he needed to be challenged. She provided 3rd-grade math pages for him and provided language arts worksheets centered around his interest in bugs and insects. He loved it and requested homework so he could do more "school" at home.

The progress Logan and the other children made in the months that followed was phenomenal. Logan was happy, challenged, and the previously frequent running incidents were reduced to minimal. I was sure to email the new director of programs for exceptional children to thank her for her involvement and all it undoubtedly took behind the scenes for this positive change to happen.

Sadly, several months later Jamie told me she would be leaving the school as one of her children required extended medical care and support. I was sad to hear this, but of course, understood. She assured me that she would pass on instructions to the new hire, and hoped that the momentum she'd built would continue. We had a big going-away party and appreciation for her before she left, which left us both in tears. We'd grown close and had worked together well. She was going to be sorely missed.

Letter to the Superintendent

Dear Sir,

I am writing you today regarding concerns I have regarding the education of my grandson, Logan, who is five years old, and currently a student in your district.

I am the grandmother, guardian, and caregiver of Logan, child of a single father, my youngest son, whose employment has made it necessary for him to be away from home a great deal of the time. I have taken care of him since he was 6 months old. Therefore, being Logan's full-time caregiver, I am responsible for what happens in his life and required to be his advocate, just as a natural parent would be.

Logan was tested and diagnosed with developmental delays when he was three years old. After this, he attended preschool in a mainstream Head Start classroom in North Polk Elementary at Fort Polk, Louisiana, where he was retested and his diagnosis changed to High-Functioning Autism (HFA), at risk for ADHD. Logan also has a Sensory Processing Disorder. While at North Polk Elementary, his IEP made him eligible to start receiving 90 minutes per day of special education, 60 minutes per week of speech therapy, and 30 minutes per week of occupational therapy in a learning center.

Through working intensively with Logan in the school setting and at home, he has made tremendous progress over the past two years. From barely talking and communicating at age three, he has become verbal and learned to read, spell, and write. While he still has occasional meltdowns, major meltdowns are rare, and he has learned to cope better with several sensory issues as well.

He has a frontal lisp, his pragmatic speech is still lacking, and his communication and social skills remain areas of concern. Some safety issues need to be addressed also, because, like many children with autism, Logan lacks a sense of danger, and can tend to impulsively bolt or elope.

When we moved from Louisiana to North Carolina I enrolled him in his current school and prepared him the best I could for the mainstream kindergarten class of Mrs. T. According to the IEP that came with him from Louisiana, he would still be receiving additional special education, speech, and occupational therapy as in his previous school.

Logan experienced problems in his new setting from the start, due to several factors: The classroom size was a lot larger, and Mrs. T. and her assistant were not able to pay sufficient individual attention to Logan. He was overstimulated, as well as confused by too many transitions in his schedule, which made it very difficult for him to settle into a routine, which is necessary for him to be successful.

Over the past months, Mr. Ron Gibson has been extremely helpful in meeting frequently with Logan's team and me to try to work out the best possible solutions to the challenges Logan faced in the mainstream setting. However, Mrs. T. and others couldn't implement the different modifications and tools suggested by Mr. Gibson consistently enough for Logan to be successful. These interventions worked flawlessly when implemented consistently at home and have made a big difference in his overall behavior, which shows that when the correct tools are utilized and modifications put in place, Logan can succeed with no resistance or further issue.

Logan continued to regress and I repeatedly requested an aide for him to help him adjust. I was told that this was not possible, and because of the continued challenges in the classroom, it was eventually decided to move Logan to a separate setting.

This was a very difficult decision for me to agree to, as I know he can be successful in a mainstream classroom, as was evidenced last year. When Logan connects with a teacher, receives appropriate attention, maintains a reasonable routine, follows a sensory diet, and uses his tools or modifications consistently, he does well and can be challenged to complete tasks and behave appropriately.

One of the main reasons I agreed to this change in his IEP was because I was promised that Ms. Kellie was going to be appointed and would be assisting Ms. M. in helping to find solutions for some of the behaviors that have kept Logan from settling into a regular classroom routine. Logan would also continue to go to KG enhancement classes each day, along with another student in his class and one of the assistants, to help integrate him back into the least restrictive setting as soon as possible.

There has been some improvement in Logan's behavior since joining Ms. M.'s class, and he likes his new teacher, her assistants, and the new setting. He is calmer and has mostly good days now, which of course is good news. There are, however, some serious concerns I have.

First, the promise of Ms. Kellie providing behavior support to Ms. M. did not materialize for whatever reason. I was very disappointed to find out "accidentally" that, after having been promised Logan and the other students in his class would be benefitting from her input, this did not happen. I feel an explanation would have been in order.

Second, the class he was to join of 11 children, including the kindergarten student who would go to enhancements with him each day, was altered unexpectedly, again without any explanation. Ms. M. has been working hard to adapt to this change and help all her new students adjust as if it were starting the school year all over again. Because of this reorganization, which must have been very difficult for the other exceptional students also, it has not worked out for Logan to attend the enhancement classes as reflected in his IEP yet.

Third, Logan tends to mimic others and is starting to pick up some of the behavior of the children in his class, who are all older, and some much older, than he is. I feel it is important that Logan can be with students his age, at least sometime each day, so he can model after appropriate and neurotypical behavior.

Fourth, Logan has not been getting the 30-minute Occupational Therapy he desperately needs regularly, nor has the sensory diet been developed that was promised, which he needs to do better in his classroom.

Fifth, his speech sessions were cut to just 30 minutes each week due to behavior problems. I was not happy about this, but I understood the reasons, and we agreed to readdress this in our next IEP meeting at the beginning of December. Logan needs to keep making progress in his communication and pragmatic speech, so he will be more ready for first grade next year.

I realize that there are reasons for everything, including understaffing, underfunding, too big a workload for those who are providing services, and decisions being made by those not as knowledgeable about the need for consistency and routine of exceptional and/or autistic children. I understand and sympathize, but I cannot accept these reasons for Logan not getting what he needs and deserves.

I feel that at this point, to start moving even moderately towards Logan being integrated back into a least restrictive environment, which he is entitled to and capable of, Logan needs extra help to address the behaviors that caused problems in the mainstream classroom, as well as some of the things he is picking up in his current situation. I am very concerned that these behaviors do not become habits, which I don't believe needs to be the case if we can intervene now.

I also feel that Logan needs a competent and knowledgeable aide to accompany him to daily enhancements, until such a time that he has learned to transition properly, behave acceptably, and benefit fully from the subjects taught.

Logan has autism, and there will always be challenges, but I am convinced that with the appropriate services, as smart as he is, Logan can learn to do well in a mainstream classroom. There are no "separate settings" in this world once Logan grows up, and we only have a small window of time to work with him to get him ready for this world. He is at his most impressionable age, and if we can provide him with the help he needs now, I know it will pay off and prevent him from needing much more costly and intensive interventions down the line.

Sir, I have expressed these concerns repeatedly over the past months without receiving the needed response, so I feel I have no other option than to turn to you and implore you to please help, so the rest of this school year will not continue to be a set of struggles for him and all concerned. I know it can be a successful year filled with progress for this amazing child, who I truly believe may surprise us all one day with what he can accomplish.

Having said this, please be assured that I am not out to point fingers, or make trouble in any way. I simply feel I must ensure that my grandson receives the kind of education and help he needs to become a well-functioning and successful person, and is provided with the same rights and opportunities that every other child is entitled to. I am not asking any more than this.

Thank you for taking the time to read this. I look forward to hearing back from you, and most of all, to Logan receiving the services he needs as per his IEP. Please be assured that I am committed to doing all I can at home to reinforce what he is learning at school, and to cooperate fully with those who are and will be working with Logan.

Sincerely and gratefully,

Ymkje Wideman–van der Laan

CHAPTER 25

Help from Jen

Meanwhile, at home, I also faced a lot of challenges with Logan's behavior and his everyday care. The demands of navigating the school situation, toilet training, getting him on a good sleep schedule, helping him manage frustrations, and keeping him safe and from eloping were starting to take a toll. Being on my own with him, with little support and few breaks to look forward to left me feeling overwhelmed sometimes. I felt very tired and alone, and I realized that I needed to ask for help.

While asking and looking around online, I came across a website offering parent support and coaching. Autism Consulting and Training seemed exactly what I was looking for. I called the number listed and scheduled a call with Jennifer Lingle, the founder. I was so excited at the prospect of having someone to talk to and get advice from regularly. That is, until I realized the cost of the different available programs. The prices were reasonable, really, but being on a very tight budget at that time, enrolling was not within reach.

Still, I could not get the thought out of my mind that I was meant to benefit from this resource. I decided to contact Jen again and ask her if she would consider trading her expertise for my editing skills. I thought it was a long shot but was elated when Jen agreed to trade six months of coaching, including ten calls with her, for me editing her blog articles.

The help she provided was terrific! We started with an intake call, after which Jen shared a list of goals and recommendations for Logan and me, a letter with recommendations for school, and an eleven-point checklist of tools I would need to succeed. Before each of the ten phone calls, I had to complete one section of the checklist. This was followed by regular emails with smaller and more specific goals to work toward.

Some of the items on her checklist I already had in place, thanks to all I learned in my previous location from the staff at Fort Polk Elementary, yet other items were still important to work on.

I cannot begin to explain how much Jen's support helped me. When I was stumped with something, I could send her an email, and she would get back to me with suggestions specific to Logan's needs. I finally felt like I had someone in my corner whom I could depend on, which made a huge difference. It helped me regain my positive perspective and restored my faith that Logan was going to be all right and grow in every aspect.

When the six months' worth of coaching ended, our

friendship and collaboration didn't. I continued to edit and work with Jen for years to come and learned so much from her in the process. Autism Consulting and Training has changed into Autism Educates since then. Jen also launched some great autism clubs on Facebook, covering behavior, social skills, and sensory issues. Check it out when you have a chance at www.AutismEducates.com.

Eleven Point Checklist: The Tools You Need to Succeed

How to improve your relationship with your child:

1. Recognize that your child is a visual learner.

- ☐ Place visual strategies throughout your home where your child can see them. Praise him for following the directions.

- ☐ Visually break down frustrating tasks for your child by using task strips (include after-school routine, cleaning up, setting the table, and homework time).

2. Create a clear behavior system.

Answer the following questions:

- ☐ What are your house rules? (Post visual rules.)

- ☐ How are you going to positively reinforce the rules? (Post rewards; i.e., sticker chart.)

- ☐ What happens if your child breaks a rule? (Post consequences.)

- ☐ What are the rules for different situations? (For example, car rules, restaurant rules, rules when with grandparents and other family members.)

- ☐ What is your action plan if your child has a meltdown in public?

3. Create a routine for you and your child.

- ☐ Get an agenda or use your phone calendar to keep track of your appointments and your child's activities.
- ☐ Write down YOUR weekly schedule.
- ☐ Write down YOUR CHILD'S weekly schedule, including therapies, school, and major activities.
- ☐ POST THIS SCHEDULE FOR YOUR CHILD TO SEE!
- ☐ Create a DAILY schedule for your child, including school, therapies, mealtimes, homework time, downtime, family time, playtime, bath time, and any other activities. Use symbols, photographs, or words, depending on your child's level.
- ☐ POST THIS SCHEDULE FOR YOUR CHILD TO SEE!
- ☐ Let your child check off each activity after it occurs.

4. Clean up clutter. Get organized!

- ☐ With your child's help, place his toys, activities, and games in containers. Label the containers. By cleaning up clutter in his bedroom and home, you are helping to create a calm, structured environment. Labeling also helps your child complete his chores because he knows that everything has a place.

5. Create structured mealtimes.

- ☐ Choose one meal to focus on, either breakfast, lunch, or dinner (dinner is recommended).

- ☐ Review mealtime rules.

- ☐ Sit down at the table and eat with your child. This provides wonderful opportunities for him to see and model appropriate manners. Mealtimes also provide communication opportunities. Model conversation with other adults at the table. Practice asking and answering questions with your child and with another adult.

- ☐ Ask open-ended questions. Teach your child how to ask open-ended questions. (For example, "Tell me about the children in your class." "How do you think we should spend our weekend together." "Today was fun because…?"

6. Encourage independence everywhere, all the time.

- ☐ The earlier you foster independence, the more successful your child will be.

- ☐ Set up an independent workstation where your child should do his homework. This workstation can also be used for independent play.

- ☐ Make sure the table and chair provide your child with proper posture. He should be able to place his feet flat on the floor. His legs should fit comfortably under the table. You may need to face the table toward a wall, to minimize distractions.

- ☐ Set up three boxes or containers. Place a familiar activity in each box. Each activity should have a clear beginning and end. Crossword puzzles, word searches, and coloring inside-the-line pictures are great activities. Legos and computer time are too open-ended for this workstation. Have your child do the activities and then place them back in each box. This is not the time to teach a new activity. Only use tasks that he can independently complete.

- [ ] When finished with all three activities, provide a reward! Have your child pick the surprise before he starts to provide an incentive for completing his tasks. The surprise does not have to be tangible. It can be reading a story or having one-on-one time with you!

- [ ] Give your child extra time to complete tasks, even if it takes a while. Sure, you can tie his shoes much faster than he can, but allow him to be successful. The only way your child is going to master a skill is if you give him the time and opportunity to do so.

7. Make time for homework and/or structured play.

- [ ] Create a homework system. Your child should complete his homework at the independent workstation. Make a list or have your child make a list of the homework tasks that he needs to complete. Let him know that there is an end in sight. As he completes each assignment, have your child check off the activity from his list.

- [ ] Try using a folder with two pockets. Write "start" on the left pocket and "finished" on the right pocket. As your child completes each worksheet or task, have him place it in the pocket on the finished side of the folder.

8. Take a moment to breathe!

- ☐ Create scheduled time to relax, even if it is sitting in silence for five minutes. Teach your child that everyone needs their space for a few minutes, including YOU!

- ☐ During this scheduled "Quiet Time," allow your child some downtime. Let him engage in activities that he enjoys, even if it is twirling a spinning top for five minutes. He needs downtime too.

9. Set up a structured time to work on social skills.

- ☐ Teach your child rules and key components to social skills.

- ☐ Role-play and have your child practice his new skill-set!

- ☐ Create social stories to help your child handle different social situations.

- ☐ Play board games or other activities that your child is interested in.

10. Is everyone on the same page?

Answer the following questions:

- ☐ Does every person involved in your child's life understand the rules and expectations?

- ☐ Is everyone aware of your child's diet restrictions?

- ☐ Is everyone fostering independence?

- ☐ Share success stories and challenges with your child's classroom teacher.

11. Respect your child's sensory needs.

- ☐ Find a replacement for inappropriate sensory-seeking behaviors (i.e., squeezing a ball or Play-Doh instead of squeezing himself or others, chewing on a chewy tube or chewy pencil topper instead of chewing on his shirt).

- ☐ Encourage movement activities (i.e., jumping on a trampoline, rocking chair, swimming, karate, kickball).

CHAPTER 26

Some Thoughts on Inclusion

I passed on the letter with Jen's classroom recommendations for Logan to Ron and the school staff in January 2012. It reflected my desires for Logan perfectly. I wanted him to be included in a general education setting as much as possible, surrounded by neurotypical peers so he could learn from them. He did mainstream for music class a few times, but the general education teachers were so unprepared for him that he ended up doing better staying in his classroom.

I have come to realize through the years that decisions on inclusion are almost always based on whether the child is ready to be included in a general setting. Of course, each child is unique, and some children do need to be in a self-contained classroom to meet their needs appropriately. Still, in many cases, we may have things backward.

Inclusion might be recommended and become more

common if rather than asking if the child is ready for inclusion, we ask ourselves, as schools and teaching staff, if we are ready to include the child.

Having worked in special education settings for many years now, I am aware of the challenges that teachers face when children with special needs join their often-overcrowded classrooms. They can barely meet the needs of the students they already have and they often lack the training to include children with autism and other disabilities. While it is often the easier solution to keep these children in separate settings, it is rarely the best for the children who have the potential to excel in inclusive settings.

Inclusion also often depends on the district and school leadership's support. In areas where inclusion is promoted and encouraged from the top down, and training and assistants are provided to the teachers, inclusion is much more common.

I will forever promote and advocate for inclusion for Logan and all children on the autism spectrum. It is important to me to see them have the best possible opportunities to learn and work alongside their neurotypical peers in the least restrictive environment. They may need considerable support to get started, but the benefits far outweigh the costs.

Unfortunately, Logan's school was not ready for inclusion, and besides nonexistent mainstreaming, the children in the self-contained special education classes were also excluded from extracurricular activities.

I was so sad to arrive at Logan's school on the first day of May 2012 to see that his class had not been included in the schedule for their annual field day activities. He and his classmates were subjected to long waits in line, which led to meltdowns and frustration. Another class of special needs preschoolers was still inside and glued to their classroom window, watching the children outside having fun. When I asked the teacher about it, she said their class had not been invited to the lineup of activities.

I was able to find and talk with a few of the other teachers, and this class was tentatively allowed to join the activities. I volunteered to stay on to help and we managed to negotiate time slots with those running the different stations. Still, it was quite chaotic for both students and staff. Afterward, when considering all that happened that day, I felt the need to write another letter to advocate for positive and lasting change.

I received a reply from the director shortly after sending my letter. She wrote:

> I am very concerned about what you have shared. While I am sure no one intended such a negative outcome, I will say firmly that I would rather not even have a field day than to have one that causes heartache for any group of students. Clearly, our goal is to engage in the best-advanced planning so that the needs of all children are anticipated and so that special activities like field day can be a source of joy and pride for everyone! We will work on this as part of our orientation for incoming staff (EC Director and Principal) as you have referenced; I believe other schools in our district must already

have some of this solid procedure implemented; however, we will look to our entire district to be sure that the needs of our special education students are being met in all field day situations. I appreciate that you are sharing this, and again, apologize that this experience was not all it could have been for Logan.

This was the beginning of further communications, and in the months that followed a group of parents of children with autism was able to form a council to work with the county toward more positive change.

Parental empowerment is an integral part of any school system, and through our newly formed Autism Parent Advisory Council (APAC), we were taking responsibility for the education of our children by assisting the schools in our county with identifying issues that impact a reasonable education for ASD children, researching successful programs from across the nation for best practices, obtaining grant funding to support these programs, and overseeing their implementation. In short, we intended to work with the board of education of the county's schools to create an award-winning, nationally recognized ASD program that could be easily replicated throughout North Carolina.

This council met with the board of education many times, and much has changed there since the year that Logan attended kindergarten. That time still serves as a reference point for me and a reminder that not being afraid to speak up for change will have an effect and improve situations. I am so proud to have been a member of this council for a short time.

Letter to the Board of Education

Dear Sir,

First, I want to thank you for your response to my inquiries and concerns earlier this school year. It has been a year wrought with change and challenge, particularly for my grandson Logan, who has autism, and his self-contained classroom.

As I mentioned in an earlier email, a lot of progress was made after Mrs. Kostan put in place a tremendous program in his setting, which turned things around from utter confusion to a productive environment, conducive to learning and progress. I could not have been more pleased. I was very sad to see her go after such a short time in Logan's class, but I understood the reasons. I expected there would again be some difficulties with yet another new teacher coming into my grandson's class—his fourth teacher this year—but overall, things transitioned fairly well. I hope with all my heart for the sake of Logan and the other students that the rest of the school year will be reasonably stable.

The reason for this letter is to pass on to you some serious concerns and observations after attending part of field day on May 1st. When I joined Logan and his class in the gym, where the activities started, I learned that the special needs classes had not been included in the lineup of activities. This resulted in a very long and difficult wait and frequently changed signals to Logan and his classmates, which was very unsettling for all of them. In the end, they did not get to participate in the tug-of-war and other games they so patiently waited for.

As they moved outside and the activities progressed, the confusion continued and one after the other promised activity was changed on the special-needs classes, which of course upset some of them, including my grandson. One other special-needs class, the four-year-olds, were not invited to participate at all and only joined the activities at the encouragement of some of the other teachers.

I am not sure of all the details on how this situation came about, but I feel that the lack of proper planning and consequent exclusion from the lined-up activities bordered on discrimination. The children did get to participate in some of the activities after lunch but there was no preparation on the part of management for full inclusion of the special needs students into these activities.

For children with autism, it is extremely important to be prepared ahead of time for changes in their routine or daily schedule, so they can adapt more easily and transition smoothly. I feel that the lack of preparation beforehand set Logan and the rest of his class up for failure rather than success.

To be frank, the contrast I have witnessed this year in the treatment of exceptional children between Logan's previous school and other schools in the area and this school is so stark that it hurts my heart. I wonder if my grandson is entitled to a free and appropriate education, why even his play is discriminated against.

I am aware that many changes are happening in our county, as well as in our school, and that there will be new hires after several resignations and retirements take place. I hope that appointing new people to these positions will signify positive progress and that our county is standing at the cusp of great change. I hope that these new appointments will be progressive, forever eliminating these backward practices of exclusion or failure to plan properly for special needs students' inclusion in every aspect of their school experience. I hope they will not only seek to promote and find solutions for more inclusive settings for each special student but that they will also raise the respect level for these very special children.

Excluding special needs students from activity days, or any activity, and/or not preparing and putting modifications and accommodations in place for them so they can successfully attend, is unacceptable to me. They are NOT second-class citizens. They deserve respect, so they grow up with self-worth through acceptance, not self-loathing through just being tolerated or shoved aside. It may seem like these children don't even notice, but I am convinced that they do, even if they cannot express their feelings like you and me. I feel it is imperative they feel valued and appreciated for who they are.

In closing, I want to thank you for reading my letter. I would appreciate it very much if this situation could be looked into, and that it will result in true and lasting change. I would be more than happy to meet with you in person and share in more detail some general observations and practical suggestions on how such situations could be avoided. I know from my contact with Mrs. H. that you, as the board of education, are equally concerned that all children's needs are met and their rights respected, including and especially those with special needs. I hope that bringing today's deplorable situation to your attention will be a catalyst to reach these goals more quickly and that this county will become a front-runner in considering the needs of their special students.

I am looking forward to your reply.

Respectfully,

Ymkje Wideman–van der Laan

CHAPTER 27

Our Move to California

Meanwhile, in California, my son had met Jill. They visited us at Christmas, and then again for Logan's birthday. My son had wanted us to move to California earlier, but we decided that it would be better to wait out the school year and then make the big move. I am so glad we did, as all the progress made during the year at Logan's school would not have been possible. Now that the school year was coming to a close, it was time to start preparing seriously.

It was going to be a big change for Logan, as he and I would be moving in with Chris and Jill initially, in preparation for me moving into my own place without him. It would be his first time living without me since he was 6 months old. He also would be starting 1st grade in a brand-new place and school.

It was also going to be a big change for me, as I would be leaving behind my daughter and her family for the first time in six years. Of course, it was important for Logan to be close to his dad again, but I experienced many and mixed emotions.

Chris arranged the moving truck and aspects of our big move, and I contacted the school in the district where Logan would be living to lay the groundwork for his next school year. Of course, much would need to be done in person when we'd get there, but at least I had a clear idea of all that we needed to bring and the process of enrolling once there.

We started packing well before moving day, and Logan got to pack his personal belongings into boxes all by himself. It helped him feel part of it, and marking the boxes with his name gave him a feeling of security.

When the moving truck finally arrived and everything was loaded, Logan walked somewhat forlorn through the empty rooms in our apartment and commented, "It's an old house now, not our new one anymore." His little mind and heart were processing this big event. Even though he could not verbalize his feelings very well, I could sense his sadness that mirrored my own.

Despite all the challenges of the past year, our little home had been a happy place, and Logan had grown tremendously. He had adjusted so well and had felt safe and secure. We'd also had many happy times with my daughter and his cousins, including sleepover weekends and weekend outings to Camp Royal, the Autism Society of North Carolina's campsite and vacation spot for families with children on the spectrum. Besides leaving our home, friends, and family, we were also leaving behind many happy memories.

I hugged him tight many times that day and spoke positively about all the fun things we were going to do the next week while staying with my daughter's family before our plane trip to see his dad. He got excited about the time he'd get to spend with his cousins, and after we locked up the house and left for my daughter's place, he was his happy self again.

CHAPTER **28**

The Plane Trip

We moved from the East Coast to the West Coast on July 15, 2012. I had felt quite anxious about taking Logan on his first long flight, and wondered how he would do standing in line before going through security and sitting still for so long.

I wanted to be well prepared, so after giving it some thought, I decided to call Raleigh-Durham Airport's customer service. When I got through to the person in charge, I explained the situation and asked if she could help make my grandson's trip as pleasant as possible by contacting airport security and asking them for special assistance. "Normally, this is only arranged for people in wheelchairs or those with physical disabilities," she explained.

However, this dear lady was aware of the challenges an autistic individual may face while traveling, as she had a family member with autism. She understood the need for assistance right away when I told her that there was a possibility my grandson would not do well in a crowd or long lines, and she went out of her way to make prior arrangements for us.

When we arrived at the Delta check-in counter, the airline manager at the desk knew we were coming and he was very accommodating, so check-in was quick. We proceeded to security, and I was happily surprised to find that the security personnel were also aware. We were allowed to go through the flight personnel security line, which helped to avoid the very long wait in line at this crowded airport. One of the security officers took our carry-on bags through for us, so I could stay with my grandson to guide him through our security check. This officer returned the bags to us once we were cleared. The security staff was extremely cordial and sensitive, and the whole procedure didn't take more than ten minutes!

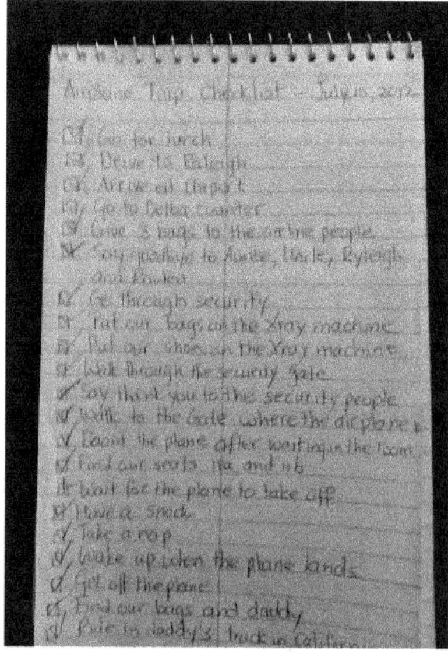

I had also prepared a simple, written-out visual checklist in my notebook for Logan to follow and check off as we completed each step of the journey, which was engaging for him and helped him know ahead of time what was coming next. We still had a bit of a wait before boarding time, so we took some good walks through the terminal. Logan was thrilled to discover some old-fashioned payphones and spent quite a bit of time "calling" different people: "Hello? Goodbye!"

Once we boarded, he was so excited! His nose was glued to the window when the airplane started taxiing down the runway, but as soon as the airplane started moving fast, he slammed it shut and didn't want to look out again until well after takeoff and the plane had stabilized. He took the sensory experience of takeoff extremely well. He held on to the seat's armrests very tightly and sat very still until the plane steadied. Once in the air, he was ecstatic to see the clouds and the world below. "Grandma, I can see the WHOLE world!" he shouted.

I had brought different activities for him, such as a small storybook about an airplane trip with reusable stickers to place on the pictures of airports and planes, and I had made sure his V-Tech games were loaded with fresh batteries, too. He hardly used those, however, as he was so fascinated with all that happened around him, and he loved eating his airplane dinner before taking a short nap, wrapped in his favorite blankie and his head on my lap.

Another concern I had was helping my grandson use the restroom on the plane, as the flush can be so loud. Due to his sensory issues, loud sounds, and especially loud toilet flushes, could get him very upset. A friend suggested not flushing until my grandson had already stepped outside the restroom, or not flushing at all and asking for assistance should that be too difficult. Thankfully, my grandson was fascinated with all the "new" things he saw in the restroom, and by using the first flushing tip, the multiple restroom trips were successful!

Once we arrived at our destination and crossed off the

last entry on my grandson's checklist, I heaved a sigh of relief. All the preparation had paid off and the whole trip went by without a hitch—and what's more, without a meltdown!

Logan's Airplane Trip Checklist

- ☐ Go for lunch
- ☐ Drive to Raleigh
- ☐ Arrive at the airport
- ☐ Go to the Delta check-in counter
- ☐ Give three bags to the airline people
- ☐ Say goodbye to Auntie, Uncle, Ryleigh, and Raiden
- ☐ Go through security
- ☐ Put our bags through the X-ray machine
- ☐ Put our shoes through the X-ray machine
- ☐ Walk through the security gate
- ☐ Say thank you to the security people
- ☐ Walk to the gate where our airplane is waiting
- ☐ Wait for our turn to get on the plane
- ☐ Board the plane and find our seats 11a and 11b
- ☐ Wait for the plane to take off
- ☐ Have a snack
- ☐ Take a nap
- ☐ Wake up when the plane lands
- ☐ Get off the plane
- ☐ Find our bags and Daddy
- ☐ Ride in Daddy's truck in California

CHAPTER 29

Passing the Baton

It had been a year since Logan arrived in California and moved in with his dad and Jill when Chris asked if I could take care of Logan for a week while he and his fiancée went on vacation. Of course, I said yes, and I looked forward to spending quality time with him. Seeing him adjust well to his new situation and make a lot of progress had made it a lot easier but I still missed being with him more, so getting a whole week with him was going to be special and a lot of fun!

Of course, I asked for any scheduling or food needs that would be helpful for me to know about during the week I would care for him. I soon received a long email from Jill, detailing everything I would need to do or should not do during my time with him. I smiled as I read it. Much of it I had passed on when Logan first moved here, and I recognized my own zeal in it. I told them not to worry and to have a great time—everything would be fine.

When I arrived at their home the day of their departure, there were another three pages of hand-written instructions. My son chuckled and joked, "Mom, did you get your book? It means she cares, Mom." "I know," I said, as I smiled back and again assured them all would be fine.

I took note of the additional meal instructions and schedule details and then put the lists away, determined to most of all have a fun time with my grandson, who was as excited as I was. We had a great week together, and he had great days at school, too. He was so proud to tell me every day that he had a "5 Star" day at school, and a "10 Reward Bucks" afternoon at his after-school program. That weekend, we had a fun-packed day together with his two cousins, and of course, as grandmas do, he got a few extra surprises for doing so well all week.

One of the greatest joys during that week was to hear him communicate his wants and needs so clearly. From not being able to express himself at all or well during his preschool and kindergarten years, he had grown into a second-grader able to share about his day, express his likes and needs clearly, and ask politely for things. He also surprised me a few times by asking me, "Remember, Grandma, when…?"

One thing he remembered was how we used to brush our teeth together after meals and before bed. That is when I taught him to use a toothbrush by himself, which was a huge sensory challenge when he was smaller. We'd start at the same time, and rinse at the same time. He promptly pulled me to the bathroom that first night and wanted to brush his teeth together with me just like we used to do, complete with giggles and laughter. It was one of the special moments we shared each evening throughout the week.

He also was quite clear on what he'd want in his lunch box each day. I referred to the list of different things he liked, so each evening I'd give him a choice of what he'd like me to pack for his next day's lunch. Most evenings he chose the preferred peanut butter and jelly sandwich, with an occasional request for the turkey ham-and-cheese roll-ups. On our last day together, however, he requested very politely to have the ham without the cheese, and nuts for a snack. I explained that he might still be hungry if that's all he'd have for lunch, and I asked him if he'd like me to put the ham on a sandwich. He was quite thoughtful and then said, "Yes!" Looking for something to put on his bread, I found some cream cheese triangles and asked him if he'd like that on his bread so it would not be so dry. He loved that idea, too, and watched me carefully as I spread it on.

This may sound silly, but looking at him watch me prepare his lunch with the most satisfied look on his face brought tears to my eyes. I recalled the times when he would melt down because I didn't make his sandwich or lunch just the way he liked it. He couldn't tell me then what he wanted. I'd have to probe, use visuals to try and find out why he was upset, and constantly work with him to help him learn to "use his words" and communicate appropriately. This was what his speech therapists had worked with him on for years, too.

That little conversation was the highlight of the week for me. I just couldn't think of a better reward for my labors of caring for him during the early years of his life.

Oh yes, and about those lists…. Routines, schedules, and

diet are very important, of course, but letting up a little and leaving room for spontaneity is okay, too. That conversation about a ham-and-cream cheese sandwich that was not on the "items for lunch" list will always be a treasured memory, and if I had stuck strictly to the routine, I would have missed it.

To those of you caring for young children on the spectrum I would like to say, hang in there, dear parents, grandparents, and caregivers! I know the challenges can be daunting and try you to your limit. I was there not too long ago. Someone then encouraged me that all the love, care, and early intervention would pay off, that it would get better with time—and it did!

You will see the fruit of your labors as you continue to work with your child, and you, like me, will stand amazed at your child's progress. It will be different for each individual because each child with autism is unique and special, but the progress you'll see! I am sure of it!

My Top Six Affordable [Early] Intervention Suggestions

If you are a parent or caregiver of a newly diagnosed child and just finished reading this book, you may feel a little overwhelmed and wonder where to start. To help make things simpler for you, here are my top six affordable [early] intervention suggestions to help you begin.

It will take time and a lot of hard work, but any—preferably early—intervention, if implemented consistently, will pay off and considerably impact your child's prognosis.

1. Make A Wish List!

The very first thing you may want to do is make a wish list of the different areas you would like to see your child progress in. This list can include things like:

- Become verbal and/or able to communicate
- Have fewer meltdowns

- Learn to use the bathroom
- Stop bolting
- Learn to read
- Sleep better
- Follow directions, etc.

Once you compile your wish list, decide on one or two areas to focus on first. Don't try to tackle everything all at once, but start with what is most important to you and your child at the time. Trying to do too much can be too overwhelming and might be too hard to keep up. Once you have decided which areas to focus on, check out the next tips and see how these could be applied and adapted to what you want to work on with your child.

2. Establish A Routine

Establishing a routine for yourself and your child can make a very big difference. Most children with autism thrive on routines, and unexpected change can often trigger meltdowns. Stick to the routine you decide on as much as possible, especially when starting to work on a particular area with your child. Consistency can make a huge difference in how fast your child will progress.

In my grandson's case, who was a hyperlexic early reader, I started writing out his daily schedule with him each morning after breakfast and before going to school, which remained a ritual for several years. The purpose for this was for him to do better transitioning from one activity to another during his school hours. If there were any foreseen changes in the schedule, his teachers would let me know ahead of time as much as possible, so I could include it in his written schedule and prepare him accordingly.

In addition to writing out his daily schedule, we used a "schedule stick" at school. His activities were on laminated, Velcro-backed little labels, which were attached to the Velcro strip on a wooden ruler. We had picture/word labels for every thinkable activity, including one labeled "Something Special" and "Surprise!" in case of an unforeseen schedule change at school, such as a canceled recess due to bad weather, for example. He loved taking off the labels and putting them in a Ziploc baggie once an activity ended, and his transitioning between activities improved dramatically within a very short time.

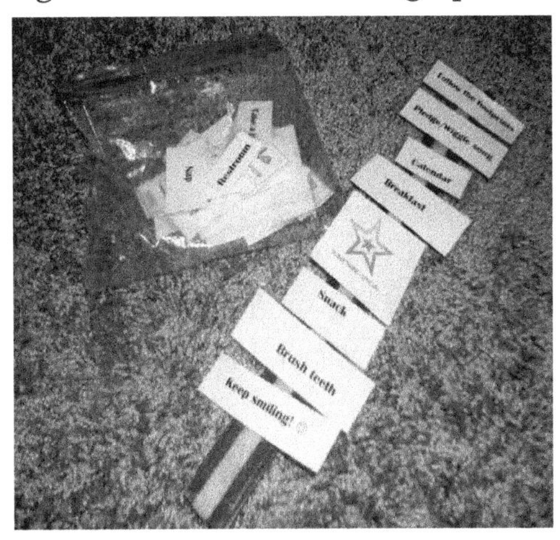

I also established a routine at home and used a picture/word schedule for the mornings, afternoons, and evenings, which he followed before and after school, and before bedtime. This helped his time at home to be a lot calmer.

Of course, sometimes things come up, both at home and at school, which makes some changes in routine inevitable. Try to prepare your child for changes as much in advance as possible, but when there is no prior warning, explain sudden changes carefully, calmly, positively, and in a fun way. "SURPRISE!!!"

3. Visuals—The Way to Go

You may have noticed that I used pictures, lists, and words to help establish a routine for my grandson. I didn't just establish a schedule and tell him about it, but also made sure to  reinforce his routine visually. This is because I learned that most children with autism are visual thinkers, and a picture can be worth more than a thousand words to them. They may not register what we say, but they will often respond to what they see and hear simultaneously.

I posted visuals throughout the apartment we lived in, and created them as needed by drawing stick figures with word captions on pieces of construction paper, writing a list on the mirror in the bathroom with a dry erase marker, or writing out a short step-by-step list for him to follow.

I also carried a dry erase marker and a laminated piece of typing paper divided into two columns with the headings FIRST and THEN with me everywhere I went. Letting him know visually (and verbally) what we were going to do "first" and "then" while running errands, for example, helped him immensely. I also used visual checklists for doctor's and dentist visits, which I downloaded from the internet and printed out for him.

Using visuals made my life (and his) so much easier, and even now, although he does not use them as intensively as before, visuals are still a great way to reinforce verbal instructions or prepare for scheduled events. Visuals are always the way to go— both at home, at school, and in the community.

4. Address Sensory Challenges

Many children on the spectrum face sensory challenges, and my grandson was no exception. Whether your child has been officially diagnosed with Sensory Processing Disorder or not, if you feel your child has sensory issues, by all means, try to find out how you can help him overcome or handle these by consulting an Occupational Therapist.

When he was younger, Logan was incredibly sensitive to certain types of socks, tough denim material, tags in shirts and pants, etc. I had no idea that many of his meltdowns were triggered by these sensitivities until his OT at school explained this to me and prepared a "sensory diet" for him. She provided me with the materials and input I needed so I could copy the therapy he received at school during his times at home, and it wasn't long before there was a marked improvement in his behavior.

For a long time, my grandson would scream when I tried to put on his socks and shoes before going anywhere. He inevitably would kick them off as soon as I managed to get them back on his feet. His OT explained that he was most likely bothered by the seams and threads inside of his socks.

I luckily found some seamless socks, and I also bought new shoes that were looser and softer. (For some other children who experience the same discomfort, sometimes turning socks inside out may work.) The change in his behavior was dramatic and nearly overnight. He kept his shoes on, and the grateful look on his face seemed to say, "Thanks, Grandma, for understanding!" Other sensory issues were also resolved and rapidly improved by following his personalized sensory diet. I will not detail here what kind of sensory exercises I did with my grandson daily, as each child's sensory needs vary greatly. The best thing to do for your child, if you suspect or know that sensory issues may be the cause of some behaviors, is to identify them and get personalized advice from a professional OT as soon as possible.

Then, don't just rely on the Occupational Therapy your child may receive once or twice a week at school, but implement any strategies your OT may recommend at home daily. In my grandson's case, regular and consistent sensory exercises desensitized him to where some of these early sensory challenges are hardly an issue anymore. He wears jeans, as well as regular socks and shoes most of the time, and if by chance a pair of socks bothers him, he can express it and change them to some that are more comfortable.

5. Capitalize on Special Interests

Many children on the spectrum exhibit specific interests, and they may even fixate on them. Whether your child is interested in dinosaurs, insects, toy cars, books, or Disney movies, try to capitalize on their interests by incorporating them into their daily routine and school subjects. It will keep

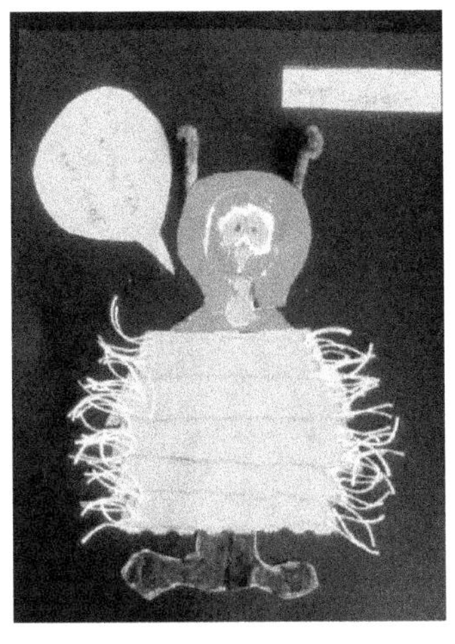

their attention and help them learn at the same time.

When 5 years old, my grandson went through a phase where he was fascinated with insects. To help him with his math, I purchased a cheap set of plastic bug counters, and I also rewarded him for good behavior with picture books about insects that I found at the Dollar store. It was also a perfect time to introduce him to Eric Carle's classic books, including *The Very Hungry Caterpillar*, which my grandson soon memorized and would quote verbatim to his peers at school and whoever else would take the time to listen to him recite a whole book. It was no surprise that he wanted a caterpillar costume for Halloween that year and that he disguised his Thanksgiving turkey as a caterpillar. His teachers also used "bug-based" rewards as incentives for completing his tasks and good behavior and even incorporated insects into his curriculum.

Whatever your child's interests are, capitalize on them and incorporate them in whatever way you can in his daily activities. His interests can be powerful motivators.

6. Teach Language

Dr. Temple Grandin said, "It's very important for the parents of young autistic children to encourage them to talk, or for those that don't talk, to give them a way of communicating, like a picture board, where they can point to a glass of milk, or a jacket if they're cold, or the bathroom."

It is extremely challenging, and there is no quick fix, to help a nonverbal child learn how to use language to communicate. Speech therapy in a public-school setting is generally limited to only several hours per week per student. If you can get input from a speech therapist and other professionals on how to reinforce the therapy your child receives at school in a home setting, by all means, try to do so. The more language your child is exposed to, the better. Talk to your child, use lots of flash cards, read books, encourage the sounding out of letters, and use the sounds your child makes by turning them into simple words.

Not all nonverbal children with autism will learn to speak, but the more you practice, and the earlier you start, the greater the chance that your child will start using speech or learn to communicate his wants and needs in other ways, such as by using a Picture Exchange Communication System (PECS), sign language, or using an iPad or other electronic communication device.

Glossary

1-TO-1 DIRECT INSTRUCTION A teacher-led instructional procedure that provides students with specific instructions regarding completion of a task, provides teacher-led practice, then independent practice including immediate corrective feedback.

ABC DATA CHART An assessment tool to gather information about what happens immediately before and after an interfering behavior occurs.

ACCOMMODATIONS Adjusting for differences; supplying a need or want in education, "accommodations" provide equal access to learning, do not substantially change the instructional level or content, are based on individual strengths and needs, and may vary in intensity or degree.

APPLIED BEHAVIOR ANALYSIS (ABA) A discipline devoted to understanding and improving human behavior by focusing on defined, observable behaviors of social significance and demonstrating a reliable relationship between the procedures employed and the resulting behavioral change.

ASPERGER'S SYNDROME (AS) A condition marked by impaired social interactions and limited repetitive patterns of behavior; motor milestones may be delayed.

ATTENTION DEFICIT HYPERACTIVITY DISORDER (ADHD)
A chronic, neurological, developmental disorder characterized by a continual pattern of inattention and/or hyperactivity, as well as impulsivity, distractibility, and forgetfulness.

AUTISM SPECTRUM A group of disorders characterized by impairments in social interaction, imaginative activity, verbal and nonverbal communication skills, and a limited number of interests and activities that tend to be repetitive. Includes Asperger's syndrome and autism.

AUTISM SPECTRUM DISORDER (ASD) A range or variety of neurological conditions characterized by widespread abnormalities of social interactions and communication, as well as severely restricted interests and highly repetitive behavior.

BEHAVIOR INTERVENTION PLAN (BIP) A detailed plan that provides step-by-step directions for addressing the child, parent, and family behavior goals.

BEHAVIORAL SUPPORT An intervention that assists an individual in learning an appropriate skill while accommodating for certain behavioral difficulties.

CHALLENGING BEHAVIOR A behavior that detracts from the task at hand. This might include acting out, aggressive behavior, rigidity, refusal to follow directions, self-injurious behavior, withdrawn behavior, etc. The behavior can be as unique and diverse as the individual exhibiting it.

DEVELOPMENTAL DELAYS A chronological delay in the appearance of normal developmental milestones achieved during infancy and early childhood.

DIAGNOSIS Identification of disorders such as Autistic Disorder; Pervasive Developmental Disorders–Not Otherwise Specified, and Asperger's Disorder. Diagnosis in the United States is most often based on the current edition of the *Diagnostic and Statistical Manual of Mental Disorders.*

DIAGNOSTIC AND STATISTICAL MANUAL OF MENTAL DISORDERS (DSM, DSM-V) The standard classification of mental disorders used by mental health professionals in the United States. It is intended to be applicable in a wide array of contexts and used by clinicians and researchers of many different orientations (e.g., biological, psychodynamic, cognitive, behavioral, interpersonal, family/systems). The DSM is now in its 5th edition.

EARLY INTERVENTION Programs for young children with special needs, from birth until the child turns three; early intervention services are authorized under IDEA Part C and may include speech therapy, occupational therapy, physical therapy, or other appropriate interventions which are typically provided in the child's home or a community setting.

ECHOLALIC OR ECHOLALIA Repeating what others say. Immediate echolalia occurs when individuals repeat words or phrases immediately after they hear them. Delayed echolalia occurs when individuals repeat words or phrases that they have heard possibly days or weeks later.

ELIGIBILITY A term used in federal legislation for special education in the United States. The term is used in the public school system. It indicates that a student has a disability and an educational need for special education supports and services.

EVALUATION A nondiscriminatory, multidisciplinary, multifaceted assessment required by IDEA before classifying a child as having a disability and providing special education services to that child.

EVIDENCE-BASED PROFESSIONAL PRACTICES A practice supported through research in peer-reviewed journals.

EXECUTIVE FUNCTION (EF) Mental processes such as working memory, behavior inhibition, mental flexibility, planning, task initiation, performance monitoring, and self-regulation.

FIRST-THEN SEQUENCE A visual sequence that outlines tasks for an individual. An initial task, usually a less preferred, or non-preferred task is specified, and following completion of that task, usually a preferred task is presented for completion.

FREE APPROPRIATE PUBLIC EDUCATION (FAPE) The concept that children with disabilities are entitled to a free and appropriate public education that meets the unique needs of the student and may occur with children who do not have disabilities or within special education classrooms. Under the IDEA, FAPE is defined as an educational program that is individualized to a specific child, designed to meet that child's unique needs, provides access to the general curriculum, meets the grade-level standards established by the state, and from which the child receives educational benefit.

FUNCTIONAL BEHAVIORAL ASSESSMENT (FBA) A process for addressing interfering behaviors exhibited by learners with ASD. FBA relies on a variety of techniques and strategies to identify the purposes of specific behavior and to help teachers and other practitioners select interventions that directly address the interfering behavior.

GENERALIZATION An individual's response in settings where no treatment or intervention has taken place. Stimulus generalization refers to performance under conditions (e.g., in other settings, with other persons) other than those that were present during the initial learning. That is, the learned behaviors are demonstrated in untrained settings.

HIGH-FUNCTIONING AUTISM An individual who is autistic with an ability to communicate, who has some social impairments, and usually an average or even high IQ.

HYPERLEXIA A hyperlexic child starts reading early and surprisingly beyond their expected ability. It's often accompanied by an obsessive interest in letters and numbers, which develops as an infant. Hyperlexia is often, but not always, part of the autism spectrum disorder (ASD).

INDIVIDUALIZED EDUCATION PROGRAM (IEP) A document that describes the student's strengths and needs, goals, and objectives, placement, and measures of the student's progress toward achieving annual goals. Each public-school child who receives special education and related services must have an individualized education program (IEP). The IEP should be a truly individualized document and should include such information as present levels of functioning, future goals, and services to be provided. By law, the IEP process must consider the need for assistive technology.

INDIVIDUALS WITH DISABILITIES EDUCATION ACT (IDEA) A law that makes available free appropriate public education to eligible children with disabilities throughout the United States and ensures special education and related services to those children.

INTERVENTION PLAN A detailed plan that provides step-by-step directions for addressing the child, parent, and family goals. The intervention plan includes (a) the instructional strategy, (b) how to provide instruction, (c) frequency and duration of instruction, and (d) when and where to provide instruction.

MELTDOWN When a student reaches the point of losing control and acts impulsively, emotionally, and sometimes explosively. Behaviors observed during a meltdown may include kicking, hitting, biting, screaming, pinching, destroying property, self-injury, and withdrawing, or becoming incapable of speaking.

NONVERBAL COMMUNICATION Those aspects of communication, such as gestures and facial expressions, that do not involve verbal communication but which may include nonverbal aspects of speech itself.

OCCUPATIONAL THERAPY (OT) A form of therapy for those with a physical or neurological disability that encourages rehabilitation through the performance of activities required in daily life.

ROUTINES Regular or customary procedures. Routines, in combination with visual schedules, assist individuals in understanding the environment and in becoming more flexible.

RULES Statements defining behavior that are permissible or not permissible in given situations or environments. Rules should be short, observable, stated positively, and easily generalized.

SENSORY PROCESSING DISORDER (SPD) The inability to modulate, discriminate, coordinate, or organize sensations effectively.

SOCIAL NARRATIVE A visually represented story or narrative that describes social situations and socially appropriate responses or behaviors. Social narratives may help the individual with ASD gain information on the thoughts and feelings of others, as well as contextual information they may have missed. Overall, social narratives can be an effective, inexpensive strategy that aids in enhanced social and behavioral understanding.

SOCIAL SKILLS Communication, problem-solving, decision making, self-management, and peer relations abilities that allow one to initiate and maintain positive social relationships with others.

SOCIAL STORY™ A story written to describe a situation, skill, or concept. Designed to provide relevant social cues, perspectives, and common responses, it is written in a specifically designed format and style. It may be used during peer social network training to provide peers with information about specific social behaviors.

SPECIAL EDUCATION Specially designed instruction regardless of the location; thus, special education is not a place or type of classroom but rather the process of ensuring that instruction is individualized.

SPEECH AND LANGUAGE PATHOLOGIST (SLP) A pathologist that provides a wide range of services, mainly on an individual basis, but also in small group settings. Speech services typically begin with initial screening for communication, speech, and/or swallowing disorders. SLPs then typically continue with assessment and diagnosis, consultation, and providing ongoing intervention and treatment.

STIMMING Behavior consisting of repetitive actions or movements of a type that may be displayed by people with developmental disorders, most typically autistic spectrum disorders; self-stimulation.

TRANSITION Movement or change from one position, subject, or location to another.

TRANSITION STRATEGIES Activities, supports, cues, or prompts put in place to assist the individual as they move through the transition process. These strategies may include visual, verbal, written, or video formats.

VISUAL SCHEDULE A procedural plan indicating the time and sequence of each operation presented in a visual format.

VISUAL SUPPORTS Any tool presented visually that supports the individual as he or she moves through the day. Visual supports might include but are not limited to visual boundaries, schedules, maps, labels, organization systems, timelines, and scripts. They are utilized across settings to support individuals with ASD.

WORK AREA An area in the home, school, or community solely used for work activities.

Recommended Books

There are many helpful autism books on the market. Below are some of the favorites from my bookshelf. All these titles are available from Amazon.com.

Thinking in Pictures: My Life with Autism expanded edition by Temple Grandin and Oliver Sacks

The Way I See It 5th edition, revised and expanded, by Temple Grandin

Ten Things Every Child with Autism Wishes You Knew revised and updated, by Ellen Notbohm

Ten Things Your Student with Autism Wishes You Knew by Ellen Notbohm

1001 Great Ideas for Teaching and Raising Children with Autism or Asperger's revised and expanded 2nd edition, by Ellen Notbohm

Uniquely Human: A Different Way of Seeing Autism by Barry M. Prizant

Everybody Is Different: A Book for Young People Who Have Brothers or Sisters with Autism by Fiona Bleach (AAPC Publishing)

Raising a Sensory Smart Child: The Definitive Handbook for Helping Your Child with Sensory Processing Issues revised and updated edition, by Lindsey Biel, Nancy Peske, et al.

The Out-of-Sync Child Has Fun: Activities for Kids with Sensory Processing Disorder revised edition, by Carol Kranowitz

Wrights Law: All About IEPs by Peter W. D. Wright, Pamela Darr Wright, and Sandra Webb O'Connor

Autism Parenting: Practical Strategies for a Positive School Experience: Over 300 Tips for Parents to Enhance Their Child's School Success by Connie Hammer

The Loving Push: How Parents and Professionals Can Help Spectrum Kids Become Successful Adults by Debra Moore, Leigh Ashman, et al.

The New Social Story Book, Revised and Expanded 15th Anniversary Edition: Social Stories by Carol Gray

Autism Is...?
Virtual Training Workshops

WORKSHOP 1

Autism Is...?

After the Diagnosis: The Basics

This 2-hour workshop offers parents, caregivers, and educators of children on the autism spectrum general information on autism spectrum disorder (ASD), support, and basic resources and strategies to help/teach autistic children.

You will learn…

- To understand autism and how it affects your child or student
- To understand the adjustment process to an autism diagnosis
- How to help your child or student
- Basic strategies and how to use simple resources to help your child or student

WORKSHOP **2**

Danger Is...?

Staying Two Steps Ahead:
Safety Considerations for Caregivers

This 2-hour workshop covers general safety considerations for parents, family members, and caregivers of children with autism.

You will learn...

- To understand how autism can impact the safety of an individual with autism
- How to be proactive in keeping children with ASD safe
- To understand how autism can impact the safety of a caregiver of a person with autism
- About other resources related to community safety for people with ASD

WORKSHOP **3**

Feelings Are...?

Behavior Is Communication

This 2-hour workshop covers behaviors that autistic children frequently exhibit, and offers suggestions to parents, caregivers, and educators on how to prevent, manage, and/or follow up on different behaviors. It also promotes understanding and compassion for children on the spectrum who often have difficulty expressing their feelings.

You will learn...

- To find and understand the reasons for frequently exhibited behaviors
- How to prevent, manage, and/or follow up on behaviors
- How to teach children to express and manage their feelings
- About the ZONES of regulation

WORKSHOP 4

School Rules Are...?

Getting Ready for Inclusion

This 2-hour workshop covers how parents, caregivers, and educators can prepare themselves and their autistic children for the first or next school year, and how to help children on the spectrum succeed while at school.

You will learn...

- How to communicate a child's needs to the school staff
- How to prepare an autistic child for school
- How to prepare and use visual supports in both the home and school setting
- How to prepare the inclusion or special day classroom

WORKSHOP 5

Manners Are...?

Open the Door for Social Skills

This 2-hour workshop looks at pragmatic communication deficits and covers several strategies to help autistic children develop appropriate social skills that contribute to their success in society.

You will learn…

- To understand why it is hard for some children to learn social skills
- To recognize the characteristics of pragmatic communication deficits
- What social skills to teach
- About scripting: role-playing for social success
- About positive reinforcement

WORKSHOP 6

Friends Are...?

Building Relationships:
What Are Fantastic Friends?

This 2-hour workshop will share strategies to help your autistic child/student foster friendships. Learning how to foster appropriate friendships can avoid problems as children on the spectrum grow older, can prevent bullying, and lead to better relationships with peers with or without autism.

You will learn…

- To understand why it is hard for autistic children to make friends
- How to handle bullying
- How to teach an autistic child to be a friend
- How to recognize problems and find positive solutions
- The importance of quality, not quantity, in friendships

To book a training workshop, contact Ymkje Wideman at autismisbooks@gmail.com. The handouts for all six workshops are available in Spanish also.

About the Author

Ymkje Wideman-van der Laan is an author, editor, and Certified Autism Resource Specialist who was born in the Netherlands. She lived and worked in countries around the globe as an educator and humanitarian before moving to the US in 2006 where she assumed the care of her then 6-month-old grandson, Logan. There were signs of autism at an early age, and Logan's diagnosis became official in 2009. She has been his advocate and has been passionate about promoting autism awareness and acceptance ever since.

Ymkje resides with her now teenage grandson in California and presents virtual and in-person autism training workshops throughout the state.

You can find out more about her books and training workshops on www.autism-is.com.

Other Books by the Author

The author wrote the _Autism Is...?_ series of children's books for her grandson, Logan, to teach him about autism, safety, school rules, feelings, manners, and friendship. Of course, there is much more to teach on each of these subjects, but the stories are great first steps and conversation starters to help autistic children learn and understand the basics, and answer their initial questions on these topics.

Logan overhears his grandma tell her friend he has autism, and he asks her, "Autism is...?" She explains to him what autism is in this beautifully illustrated story. Children with autism face many challenges, and they are often aware of and question their autism. Of course, each child is unique, and you may or may not wish to explain the term autism to your child at a young age. But if you do, this book can help make it easier for you, as it did for the author when explaining autism to Logan. His inquisitive mind wanted to know, and once he read this story, even before it was illustrated, he was happy with this positive explanation and answer to his question.

Logan runs to a busy street and nearly has an accident! Once safely back inside, his grandma talks about the meaning of danger and teaches him ten important danger rules. Children with autism often lack a sense of danger, and it can be difficult to teach them safety rules. Her grandson was no exception. *Danger Is...?* struck a chord with him, and after reading the story with him repeatedly, he started referring to it often. The author also created a Danger Rules key ring for him. Visually and verbally reviewing the Danger Rules on his key ring regularly, especially before going out, reinforced safety even more and helped keep him safe. She hopes this book can contribute to keeping other children with autism safe, too.

Logan does not finish his tasks at school, so he must do a lot of homework. After his grandma reads his daily report, she teaches him some important school rules to help him do better. Sticking to and focusing on a task, staying seated, and transitioning from one activity or place to another while in school can be challenging for children with autism. It certainly was for Logan when he started attending school. To help reinforce the rules he was learning at school, the author wrote _School Rules Are...?_ and made some simple illustrated visual supports to go along with each rule. Logan soon caught on, and Good Eyes, Good Ears, Good Hands, Good Feet, Good Voice, Good Friends became household words. The author hopes _School Rules Are...?_ with its bold and bright illustrations can help do the same for other children on the autism spectrum.

Logan sees his grandma wipe away a tear and asks her why there is water on her face. She talks with him about feelings, and teaches him _The Feelings ABCs_. Children with autism often do not sense the feelings of others, and can have difficulty recognizing or relating to abstract emotions. The author wrote _Feelings Are...?_ to help her grandson learn about emotions. Reviewing _The Feelings ABCs_ often was a great first step in helping him learn to recognize and respect the feelings of others more. She hopes this book will also be helpful to other children with autism.

Logan bumps into a customer while out shopping. His grandma asks him to apologize and later teaches him about good manners by making a list with him of the most important ones. The author later put them to rhyme and included them in this book, _Manners Are...?_ She found that

posting a Good Manners Chart, and offering a Good Manners Certificate after her grandson filled up the chart with stickers, was a great incentive and visual way to reinforce manners that needed focus at any given time. A sample chart and certificate are included in the back of this book, which you can cut out, photocopy, or laminate if you wish. Of course, there are many more manners than the ones included in *Manners Are...?* but these were what Logan needed to learn and focus on first. The author hopes that they can be a good start for other children with autism too and that this book will make it just a little easier for you to teach them.

Logan has trouble with sharing and teases a friend. His grandma teaches him how to be a good friend with some fantastic friendship rules. Non-autistic children usually learn social skills naturally and in a spontaneous way, by watching and mingling with everyone around them, but children with autism may need to learn these skills in a more tangible way, through social narratives, role play, and other means. Of course, this book is by no means a comprehensive manual on how children on the autism spectrum can nurture friendships, but the author hopes that the different "friendship rules" in *Friends Are...?* can be a springboard for conversation, as they were for her and her grandson. There is a Word List and Fantastic Friendship Rules Checklist at the back of the book to help teach children on the autism spectrum some of the important social skills needed for developing good friendships.

All books except *Feelings Are...?* are also available in Spanish. *Autism Is...?* is also available in Arabic, Dutch, Thai, and Turkish.

(Available at www.autism-is.com and on Amazon)